The Principle of the Integral Good

by Fr. Chad Ripperger

Cover by Ryan Grant

Copyright © Chad Ripperger 2018
Sensus Traditionis Press

In honorem Reginae Angelorum et in gratitudine
Coemgeno et Stephianna pro adiumento librum scribere.

Table of Contents

Abbreviations	vii
Acknowledgments	viii
Introduction	ix
Chapter 1: The Principle Itself	1
I. Different Kinds of Good	5
II. Human Psychology in the State of Fallen Nature and the Principle	6
Chapter 2: Morality	9
I. Fonts of the Moral Act	10
II. Application of the Principle to the Fonts in General	12
III. Application of the Principle to Morality in Some Specific Cases	13
Chapter 3: Beauty, Movies and Music	17
I. Distinctions of the Goods.	17
II. Convertibility of the Beautiful with the Good	19
III. The Attributes of Beauty	21
IV. Movies	28
V. Music	30
Chapter 4: Ecclesiology	41
I. A Short History of a Problem	41
II. The Ecclesiastical Response to the "Branch" Theory	42
A. The Response of Catholic Theologians	42
B. The Response of the Magisterium	43
III. The Four Causes of the Church	48
IV. Principle of the Integral Good in Relation to the Mark of Unity	50
A. God as an Integral Cause	50
B. The Catholic Church as Caused by God	51
V. Further Conclusions	56
Chapter 5: Evolution	59
I. Initial Observations	59
II. Some Thomistic Citations in Relationship to Creation	64
III. The Principle of the Integral Good in Creation	69

| Conclusion | 77 |
| Bibliography | 79 |

Abbreviations

The following abbreviations are used in this text along with those abbreviations in use in standard English. Texts of Saint Thomas:[1]

Comm. de anima	*In Aristotelis Librum de Anima Commentarium*
Comp. Theol.	*Compendium Theologiae*
De anima	*Quaestiones Disputatae de Anima*
De malo	*Quaestiones Disputatae de Malo*
De Pot.	*Quaestiones Disputatae de Potentia*
De Ver.	*Quaestiones Disputatae de Veritate*
In Ethic.	*In Decem Libros Ethicorum Aristotelis ad Nicomachum Expositio*
Meta.	*In Libros Metaphysicorum*
Quod.	*Quaestiones Quodlibetales*
Sent.	*In Quatuor Libros Sententiarum*[2]
SCG	*Summa Contra Gentiles*
ST	*Summa Theologiae*

Other texts:

CCC	*Catechism of the Catholic Church*[3]
CED	*Catholic Encyclopedia Dictionary*[4]
OCE	*Catholic Encyclopedia*[5]
SSP	*Summary of Scholastic Principles*[6]

---

[1] All translations of St. Thomas are the author's own unless otherwise noted.

[2] Citations from the *Sentences* contain first the book number, then the abbreviation, followed by location within the book.

[3] Editio typica, Libreria Editrice Vaticana, 1997.

[4] The Gilmary Society, New York, 1941.

[5] The Gilmary Society, New York, 1913.

[6] Loyola University, 1951.

Acknowledgments

I would like to express my appreciation for the ongoing encouragement from Hugh Owen, in relationship to our discussions regarding evolution, the fruits of which are evident in the chapter on evolution. I have great gratitude towards Leo Severino whose close reading of the text provided many points of clarification. A special thanks is due to Fr. Dan McElheron regarding the chapter on ecclesiology. In relation to grammatical points, I am indebted to Victoria Cervantes, who took time out of her very busy schedule to offer corrections. May God reward them all. Finally, I thank my parents whose piety and devotion to the teachings of the Roman Catholic Church manifested itself in the sound catechetical teaching that I received as a child.

Introduction

When one observes the theological and philosophical collapse among many members of the Church, even some of the higher levels of the Magisterium, as the result of centuries of philosophical and theological intellectual decay, one is struck by the lack of rational principles governing the reasoning process in philosophy and theology.[7] This is nowhere more evidenced than in relation to the principle of the integral good as it governs theological discussions in key areas of morality, ecclesiology and cosmology. The resulting confusion among the various members of the Church regarding key doctrinal questions has lead to widespread error. For this reason, it is necessary to discuss in detail the principle of the integral good so that it can be properly understood and applied.

The application of a principle in concrete requires several things to come together in order that it may be done properly. The first is one must understand the terms of the principle itself. Without a proper understanding of those terms, the formulation of the principle will not seem self-evident. Second, one must know the proper formulation or various formulations of the principle to understand it in depth. Third, one must have a proper grasp of the circumstances in order to apply the right principle properly. Fourth, one must have sufficient intellectual habits to be able to apply the principle in the concrete. Therefore, this book will follow the following format: 1) discussion of the principle, some of the revelant terms as well as the various formulations of the principle of the integral good; 2) a discussion of the application of this principle in various areas of philosophy and theology while noting the circumstances in those two sciences, viz. in the areas of morality, ecclesiology and evolution.

Lastly, the author admits that this book will appeal neither to the scholar nor to the layman. As to the scholars, they will be perceived all sorts of gaps in the discussion which could be filled out in a much longer book. In response, what can be said is that this book is highly enthymematic, in the sense that when a scholar reads it, he is going to have to bring with him a lot of philosophical and theological background. As to the layman, the book might seem a bit outside his scope of

---

[7]This reality was noted extensively in the discussion of evolution in this author's work *The Metaphysics of Evolution*.

understanding. The hope of the author is that the scholar will give it an honest read with the proper background and the layman will do the research necessary to fill in his own background so that he can make an honest read of the text.

Chapter 1: The Principle Itself

In the work called "The Divine Names" by Dionysius the Areopagite,[1] we read, "In fine, Good cometh from the One universal Cause; and evil from many partial deficiencies."[2] This principle became widely accepted during the Middle Ages and in the entire Latin tradition. The principle is normally formulated as: Bonum est ex integra causa, malum ex quolibet defectu.[3] The difference between the historical formulations and the one by Dionysius is that for Dionysius the good has one universal cause, viz. God. The historical formulation does not include God necessarily but observes that the good must have an integral cause in general. These two formulations are not at variance: any good thing will have all necessary secondary causes which are required to make the thing integral so that it does not lack anything due to its being, as all secondary causes by definition act by virtue of the one primary cause, viz. God.

When we read St. Thomas, we notice that his formulation of the principle of the integral good changes slightly to emphasize certain

---

[1] It is commonly held that the name Dionysius does not refer to the disciple of the Apostle, which was thought for some time after the work came out. It is, rather, the product of a later writer.

[2] *On the Divine Names*, c 4.

[3] The good is from an integral cause, evil from any defect whatsoever.

aspects of the principle. He does give the basic formulation in various locations.⁴ In one location, he formulates it this way: "the good, according to Dionysius, is caused from one whole cause; but from a single defect arises evil."⁵ There are two things to observe in this formulation. The first is the unity of all the causes or what may be referred to as the whole cause. In other words, it is not merely a consideration of each of the individual causes (i.e. taken together as a whole), but that they must come together as a unified cause. The second is that evil arises from a single defect. By defect here we mean something that is lacking that would complete the being in a manner that is suited to its nature. For example, we would say that a man suffers a physical evil because he is missing one arm. But this must be distinguished from a lack of a perfection which is not necessarily due to the nature of the thing. For example, the fact that a dog lacks the faculty of speech does not cause us to consider it an evil because the nature of a dog is such that it is not intended to enter into rational discourse. However, if the dog were unable to bark, we would say that there is a physical evil which the dog has suffered. The primary point is that it is a single defect, i.e. it only takes one defect or lack of being that is proper to a thing or that ought to be there, to render the whole bad or evil. The good is only achieved when there is no defect, i.e. when there is nothing lacking to the thing in relationship to those things that are proper or due to the nature of the thing.⁶

In the *Prima Secundae* of the *Summa Theologiae*, we see this formulation: "the good truly is from a total and whole cause."⁷ The use of the word *tota* in Latin indicates that it is not only a fact that all of the singular parts that go into making up the whole of the being are in fact present and good, but that the being is complete, i.e. in its totality everything necessary and proper to its being is present. This also connects

---

⁴ST II-II, q. 79, a. 3, ad 4; ST II-II, q. 92, a. 2, ad 1; ST III, q. 90, a. 2, ad 4; De Ver., q. 25, a. 5, ad 5; De Malo, q. 4, a. 1, ad 13; De Malo, q. 16, a. 6, ad 11; Sent. Libri Ethicorum, l. 2, c. 7, n. 2. See also SSP, p. 198 and p. 232f.

⁵IV Sent., d. 16, q. 1, a. 1a, ad 3: Bonum, secundum Dionysium, causatur ex una integra causa; sed ex singulis defectibus consurgit malum.

⁶See also De Ver., 28, a. 3, ad 15 and De Malo q. 2, a. 1, ad 3.

⁷ST I-II, q. 19, a. 7, ad 3: Bonum vero ex tota et integra causa. See also ST I-II, q. 71, a. 5, ad 1.

us to the observation above that there is a unicity in the causation insofar as all of the parts have to come together in some form of unified causation.[8] In the *Secunda Secundae*, another formulation provides a better sense of this: "for something to be good, it is required that everything rightly concurs."[9] When the various causes of a thing come together, they must come together in a suitable manner such that they are able to cause the thing together in a rightly ordered way. Another way to look at this is if, for example, two distinct causes came together to create a statue, those two causes must concur, i.e. come together in such a manner that, as individual causes, they do not contradict each other in relationship to what they cause in the thing that is caused. So with the statue, the artist who gives form to the clay must have the proper material provided to him by the seller of the clay. If the clay is defective or contains elements that are contrary to what the artist wants to do with the clay, then the statue will not be produced in a manner that is integrally good.

St. Thomas, in his *Questiones Disputatae de Malo*, formulates it in such a manner that he gives us another aspect to the principle which is important: "many are required to the good, which is perfected from the whole and integral cause, than in relation to evil, which occurs from a singular defect."[10] In this particular formulation, what is being stressed is that many things are required to come together in order for the good to be achieved. St. Thomas is juxtaposing evil which occurs from a single defect whereas the good occurs only when *many* things come together in the bringing of the thing into existence.[11]

If we consider this principle looking at it from the point of view of evil, certain formulations and uses of the principle in St. Thomas become important for consideration. We have already seen that evil is

---

[8] This will become particularly important in the discussion of ecclesiology and evolution.

[9] ST II-II, q. 110, a. 3: aliquid sit bonum, requiritur quod omnia recte concurrant.

[10] De Malo, q. 10, a. 1: plura requiritur ad bonum, quod perficitur ex tota et integra causa, quam ad malum, quod relinquitur ex singularibus defectibus.

[11] In relation to this discussion of evolution and ecclesiology, there will be a longer discussion of how God as a singular cause still fulfills this particular aspect of many things coming together.

constituted by a single defect.[12] In the first book of his commentary on Peter Lombard's *Sentences,* he observes that one "knows evil, since the notion of evil consists in defect."[13] The *ratio mali* or notion of evil indicates that the very conceptual understanding of evil is rooted in the fact that there is a defect. A defect is some kind of privation that is due to a thing.[14] A privation is "the lack of a good that is due to a nature"[15] (i.e. the nature of the thing), which is distinguished from a "mere negation, i.e. the simple absence of something not due[16] to or not needed to a nature".[17] This distinction we saw above insofar as if a particular perfection or good is not present to something that does not by its nature require that thing to be integral, it is merely a negation and not a privation.

In another location, St. Thomas makes this observation: "since evil is not able to be whole, except as it corrupts the entire good, which having been corrupted, that being is corrupted which is able to be the subject of evil."[18] What St. Thomas is observing here are two things. The first is that evil is not able to be whole and by that he means an existing thing cannot be entirely evil. For evil to be complete, it would have to corrupt the entire good which would also mean the ontological good, i.e. the thing would simply go out of existence. In the *Prima Pars*, St. Thomas makes the observation that "if evil is whole, it destroys itself, since the destruction of every good (which is required to the wholeness of evil) removes also

---

[12] See also ST I-II, q. 18, a. 4, ad 3 and De Malo, q. 2, a. 11, ad 1.

[13] I Sent., d. 36, q. 1, a. 2, ad 3: Et ita cognoscit malum, cum in defectu ratio mali consistat.

[14] II Sent., d. 30, q. 1, a. 2: malum nomen privationis est.

[15] Wuellner, *A Dictionary of Scholastic Philosophy*, p. 246.

[16] By "due" is meant that the being by nature requires or calls for it or that it ought to be there.

[17] Ibid.

[18] II Sent., d. 34, q. 1, a. 1, ad 4: quia non potest esse malum integrum, nisi corrumpatur omne bonum: quo corrupto corrumpitur illud ens quod mali subjectum esse potest. See also: IV Sent., d. 44, q. 3, a. 1a, ad 2 and ST I, q. 49, a. 3.

the evil itself, whose subject is the good."[19] The second is that evil cannot corrupt the entire good insofar as evil always resides in some subject. By this we mean that evil is always a privation in some existing subject or good.[20]

To sum up, we may say that (1) for a thing to be good, *all* of the causes of a thing must *come together* in some form of union to bring about the *good* thing. (2) A being is good when *all* aspects of its being that are *due* to it are present. (3) Something is rendered *evil* when there is *any defect whatsoever*, i.e. something becomes evil when there is something lacking in the being of a thing that should be there.

I. Different Kinds of Good

The good is defined as: that which all things desire.[21] Philosophers observe that there are three kinds of goods.[22] The first is called the ontological or metaphysical good, which refers to the existence of a thing. To exist is a good thing;[23] not to exist is a bad thing. In this respect, anything that exists, even demons and the damned, are said to be good, ontologically speaking.

The next is what is called the physical good. Sometimes this kind of good is called natural, insofar as it is good for a thing to have all of those things that are proper to its nature, e.g. it is a natural or physical good that one possesses all of one's fingers. It is physically bad for a person to lose one or more of his fingers.

The last kind of good is called the moral good, which pertains to the rational creature which has the capacity to grasp God's intention

---

[19] ST I, q. 49, a. 3: Si malum integrum sit, seipsum destruet, quia destructio omni bono (quod requiritur ad integritatem mali), subtrahitur etiam ipsum malum, cuius subjectum est bonum.

[20] Existence is a good, as we shall see later.

[21] Aristotle, *Nicomachean Ethics*, l. 1., c. 1 (1094a3).

[22] The various distinctions among goods can be found in Wuellner, *A Dictionary of Scholastic Philosophy*, p. 117-119 and Coffey, *Ontology*, p. 174-191.

[23] St. Augustine, *Confessions*, VII, 12; ST I, q. 5, a. 1-3; I Sent., d. 8, q. 1, a. 3; De Ver., q. 21, a. 1 and 2; SCG II, c. 41 and SCG III, c. 20. See also SSP, p. 48 (n. 181).

about his own nature as well as to foresee the effects of his acts and assume responsibility by means of voluntary choice. Spiritual goods are also considered part of this kind of good, as they are counter distinguished from the physical goods, as we see Christ observe that it is better to enter heaven with one eye than into hell with both.[24]

II. Human Psychology in the State of Fallen Nature and the Principle

Many have a hard time making proper distinctions between these three kinds of good and we have to ask ourselves why. Even Christ had to make this distinction for the Apostles.[25] We know this distinction between physical and moral goods naturally by virtue of the fact that we suffer physical evils often for the sake of the moral good. We go to war to secure the common good of a nation because we are willing to die (loss of the natural good of human life) in order to achieve the common good (the natural and moral good of society).

So why do people tend to confuse natural goods with moral goods? A classic example is fornication in which a person after experiencing the pleasure of fornication (a natural good), over the course of time and by repeated acts of fornication, begins to judge that it is morally acceptable to do so (moral good). Another example which is rife within the psychological community is the belief that masturbation is a good thing for human beings.

Why does this occur that people mistake natural for moral goods? The essential reason is that when people experience the physical pleasure or the emotional delight of a natural or physical good, the possible intellect[26] when judging the moral content of the thing which causes us pleasure or delight is precipitated into thinking that the thing is greater

---

[24]Matthew 5:29; 18:8 and Mark 9:47. The possessing of both eyes is a physical good, whereas entering heaven is a moral good.

[25]This distinction is at the root of Christ's discussion in Mark 7:18f as well as John 9 in Christ's discussion of the man born blind is not the result of sin. In other words, blindness is a physical evil, whereas sin is a moral evil.

[26]Regarding the definition and nature of the possible intellect, see Ripperger, *Introduction to the Science of Mental Health*, passim but especially, vol. I, chpt. 2.

than it is.[27] In other words, when reason looks at the natural good and the pleasure or delight arising from it in the imagination, its judgment is drawn to excess in the thinking that the thing is better than it actually is.[28] This precipitation causes the person to erroneously judge that it is morally acceptable and results in him thinking a thing is morally good which is only naturally or physically good. When this mistake is repeated often, the possible intellect is habituated in such a manner that it develops an intellectual vice so that reason is inclined to judge the thing falsely on a habitual basis. This is what happened, for example, in the United States during the 1960s. At that time, it was a commonly held that fornication was immoral. However, over the course of time, as a result of the free love movement and frequent fornication, people began to think that fornication is morally acceptable. It has become so entrenched now that it is considered to be conventional wisdom insofar as people are counseled to cohabitate prior to marriage.

As people's subtlety of judgment becomes affected by the intellectual habits that are contrary to the truth as a result of their judgment being precipitated, over the course of time the false judgments begin to spread into other areas relating to the various kinds of goods. It is for this reason that we will discuss how the principle of integral good has collapsed in the discussion of morality, ecclesiology, as well as creation theology.

---

[27]This mechanism is discussed at length in Ripperger, *Introduction to the Science of Mental Health*.

[28]This is also true of the sorrow or pain that arises out of the presence of evil. It can cause the intellect to judge that something is worse than it is or not as good as it is.

Chapter 2: Morality

When one reads various works from the history of morality, the entire Catholic moral tradition talks of three fonts of the moral act. A font is a thing from which something flows and so it may be said that the fonts of the moral act are those things which determine whether what the will chooses is morally good or bad. In other words, the fonts are the things chosen by the will and the will becomes good or bad by virtue of what it chooses. In modern philosophy, there is a great deal of discussion about how the person has the power of self determination by what he chooses.[1] So a person can determine himself to be a good person by choosing what is truly good whereas a person who chooses evil renders himself evil in the process. This occurs because the will, in the process of choice, directs itself to the good or evil that it chooses. It is contrary to right reason to assert that a person who has full deliberation in choosing something good or evil does not become good or evil in that process. This follows from the fact that the form in the intellect contains what the person chooses and that form passes over into or resides in the will when it chooses that object. In other words, the will unites itself to the object proposed by the intellect in choice in such a manner that the form as conceived by reason enters into the will by its choice. This is why the entire moral tradition

---

[1] This is nowhere more manifest than in the writings of St. John Paul II, especially his work *The Acting Person*.

is clear that sin is in the will.²

I. Fonts of the Moral Act

There are various acts of the will other than choice but they all culminate in the act of choice, in which the various fonts come together in a single object which is proposed to the will for choice.³ The three fonts are the object, the end and the circumstances. The object of the moral act is the proposed exterior act as conceived by reason and is sometimes called "the means" since it is the means by which the end is obtained, e.g. a man considers stealing a car. Stealing a car is a proposed exterior act which reason conceives the possibility of doing in order to obtain the car. The end is the intention or the reason the person performs the moral act or object. So in this case, the man's intention is to have ownership of the car which he desires. The circumstances are those things standing around the exterior act. Some circumstances make the act worse, e.g if the car was owned by his father as opposed to a complete stranger. The fact that he would steal his own father's property increases the heinousness of the act.

There are seven different kinds of circumstances. The first is *who* (*Quis*) which denotes a special quality of the person performing the act, e.g. if someone uses Our Lord's name in vain, it is an offense against the Second Commandment but if it is done by a priest who has dedicated his life to God, it is worse. The next circumstance is *In What Way* or *How* (*Quomodo vel Qualiter*). This circumstance describes the quality of the act, e.g. if a man decides to kill another man, the fact that he would kill him in a painless way is not as bad as if he killed him slowly by torturing him to death. The third circumstance is *By What Aid* (*Quibus Auxiliis*). It is because of this circumstance that many moralists are calling into question certain forms of vaccination which involve the use of fetal stem cell lines to create the vaccination. The fact that the vaccination is derived from an illicit means indicates that use of the vaccination, as a general rule and without a proportionately grave reason, renders that particular instance

---

²For example, among others see ST I-II, q. 74, a. 1; ST II-II, q. 20, a. 2; De Malo, q. 7, a. 1, ad 16 and Prummer, *Manuale Theologiae Moralis*, vol. I, p. 263, n. 383.

³This was part of the discussion in this author's work, *The Morality of the Exterior Act*.

of vaccination immoral.

The next circumstance is *Where* (*Ubi*). This indicates the location of the act to be performed. So if a teenager is given a legitimate command from his parents to not go over to a friend's house who is bad moral company, if the teenager goes to the house, it makes his act bad. This follows from the fact that he has gone to a place which his parents have legitimately forbidden. The fifth circumstance is *When* (*Quando*) which denotes the time when the act is to take place. A common example given in the moral manuals is in relation to a curfew; so if the parents place the restriction on the teenager that he cannot go to his friend's after 10 PM, if he does so, the circumstance of *when* renders what he does bad.

The next circumstance is *Why* (*Cur*) which is the end for which the action is done. St. Thomas observes that the end is a circumstance to the exterior act but is given special consideration as a separate font because it is the motivation for the choice of the object as well as a determining factor in looking at the circumstances. The reason why the man above stole the car (object) is for possession of the car (end). If he did not want to possess the car, he more than likely would not have stolen the car. The end also determines how the circumstances are often judged. So if the teenager decides to be rebellious and to get back at his parents, he may choose to go to his friend's house after 10 PM on purpose. In other words, he intentionally goes after a time when the curfew is in place in order to show his parents that he does not think he has to follow their commands.

The last circumstance is *What* (*Quid*) and *About What* (*Circa Quid*). This circumstance was often misunderstood by some contemporary moralists but it specifically refers to a quality of the object of the exterior act. That last sentence needs some unpacking. Every moral act acts upon something, e.g. stealing is the act but the car is the object which undergoes the act of stealing. One cannot steal nothing; one can only steal something. Another example is throwing a baseball; the baseball is the object of the act of throwing. This circumstance indicates that there is a quality about the object, such as the baseball or car, which affects the goodness or badness of the act. For example, if the thief were to steal a car that was a rare car and as a result is worth a lot of money, then it would be worse than if he stole a car that was 30 years old and in disrepair.[4]

---

[4] A full treatment of the fonts can be found in just about any sound moral manual but also this author's work, *The Morality of the Exterior Act*.

II. Application of the Principle to the Fonts in General

When the fonts of the moral act are considered in light of the principle of the integral good, one discovers several important things. The first is that all of the fonts must be good when they come together in the will for choice, otherwise, the whole act is rendered bad.[5] In other words, since evil is from any defect whatsoever, if what the will chooses is not integrally good but contains a defect or evil on one or more of the fonts, then the will becomes evil for making that choice. If a person does a morally good act but for a bad end, what he does is bad. A common example in the moral tradition is the man who gives alms to the poor. It is possible that a man who is wealthy would give a significant amount of money to help the poor overcome their destitution and need, which is a good thing. However, if he does it for the sake of vainglory, i.e. he does it so that people will see him doing it and think he is good, then giving the money for that reason is evil. Here we are reminded of the discussion in the previous chapter: just because we can, by an act of judgment, isolate the giving of the alms from the bad intention, does not mean that the act is not evil. It must always be remembered that all of the fonts come together in the act of choice so what the person is willing is, in fact, evil since he is willing the vainglory even though it is by a good means.

Laboring under the effects of Original Sin, people too often tend to specifically ignore the evil in one of the fonts in order make it possible to will the action. However, even the ignoring of the evil is itself part of choice and therefore is culpable. The reason for pointing this out is that in the modern context, people are often justifying their evil choices or exculpating themselves by denying the principle of the integral good as it applies to moral actions. How often it is it said, "what I did is not evil because my intention was to help the person." While the end or intention may be good, that does not change the quality or character of the action

---

[5]The application of the principle of the integral good to moral acts enjoys a unanimous consensus among sound Catholic theologians throughout history. Here are a few citations: Wuellner, *Summary of Scholastic Principles*, p. 232 (n. 232): an act is good if its whole cause is good; it is evil from any defect. The act in other words must not violate any factor of the norm of morality either in the object of the act, the intention of the agent, or intrinsic circumstances"; ST I-II, q. 18, a. 1; OCE under *good* (vol. VI, p. 639); Davis, *Moral and Pastoral Theology*, vol. 1, p. 54; Ramires, *De Actibus Humanis*, p. 486 and McHugh and Callan, OP, *Moral Theology*, Vol. 1, p. 27-28.

one performs. When taking examples to extremes, people can often see the principle as operative a little easier, so, e.g., if a man were to kill another man because the man was in pain from a limp when he walked, regardless of the intention, we would say that the intention did not change the fact that killing the man for that reason is not justified. It is for this reason that the entire Catholic moral tradition has said: the ends do not justify the means. For this reason, for example, one is not permitted to bomb innocent civilians during war, to rob Peter to pay Paul, or to lie in order to avoid suffering punishment.

III. Application of the Principle to Morality in Some Specific Cases

Many would admit that the modern context has resulted in a serious decline not just in what moderns are choosing but even in their ability to discern what is morally right and wrong objectively in specific kinds of cases.[6] The first kind of example has to do with the circumstance *About What.* In a *petitio* to the *Propagandi Fidei*,[7] the question was asked whether Catholics could swear on and kiss an heretical Bible. The question is a legitimate one, even back at the time when the question was asked because Catholics in the United States were being asked to swear on Protestant bibles when they were sworn in as witnesses in court. The *Propagandi Fidei* answered that one was forbidden

---

[6]Without going too far afield, it should be pointed out that modern man seems to labor under an inability due to intellectual as well as moral vices to discern the difference between what St. Thomas calls a circumstance and condition. A circumstance stands outside of an act and is accidental to it, whereas a condition enters into the very substance of the act and determines the moral species of what one is doing. For example, we see this with euthanasia. St. Thomas observes that killing a man is penal by nature and so to kill someone who is not guilty of a capital crime lacks the proper condition of the person's grave and heinous guilt. So to euthanize a human being because he is suffering is to fail to realize that suffering and pain are not penal and neither are not a sufficient condition to put someone to death. The discussion of the differences between circumstances and conditions is found in this author's work, *The Morality of the Exterior Act.*

[7]The *Propagandi Fidei* was a dicastery in Rome charged with the responsibility of addressing questions pertaining to the Catholic Missions and the propagation of the faith.

to do so.[8] The question is why? The answer is fairly simple but easily missed. Protestant bibles often contain error and lack the canonical books proper to the Catholic Scriptures. That being the case, the Protestant bible (the object of the exterior act of placing your hand on and swearing to God in relation to) contained errors. Since the principle of the integral good states that all of the fonts of the moral act must be good in order for the action to be morally good, one is committing an evil by swearing on a text which contains errors (defects). Technically the circumstance of *About What* is evil due to the errors and so one cannot use it to give testimony to the truth of the statements before God.

This is the same reason one is forbidden to reverence texts which are considered sacred in other faiths since only the Catholic faith and Scriptures are integrally good, i.e. good in all their aspects. The argument is often proffered that the sacred texts of other sects contain truth. This is without doubt but that is not a reason to reverence them; recognize the truths, yes, but not reverence the texts. Reverencing these sacred texts also means one is reverencing the error as well. When one analyzes the fact that, for example in kissing a sacred text of a sect which is not Catholic, one also has his lips joined to something which is erroneous as well. To make the psychological distinction, i.e. to try to distinguish the kissing as pertaining only to the truth, denies the physical reality of having one's lips to what is erroneous and offensive to God. Since the principle of the integral good requires that our acts be good in ALL of their parts, the principle does not foresee or allow psychologically separating parts out in order to render the act good.

Another very common example is approbation given to what is called *communicatio in sacris* with non-Catholics. The Holy Office[9] pointed out that:

> the Council of Carthage forbade praying and singing (psallendum) with heretics. The Supreme Congregation stated that participation in schismatic and heretic worship is "universally prohibited by natural and divine

---

[8]*Collectanea S. Congregationis de Propaganda Fidei*, vol. I, p. 432, n. 739, ad 2 (1820).

[9]The Holy Office was charged with the responsibility of ensuring doctrinal integrity within the Church. The name of the dicastery was later changed to the Congregation for the Doctrine of the Faith.

law...[from which] no one has the power to dispense ...[and with respect to this participation] nothing excuses." Those who so participate must seek absolution in the sacrament of penance.[10]

The Holy Office went on to say that as for *communicatio in divinis*[11] with schismatics and heretics, it is "constantly and uniformly forbidden." In other words, it was a moral teaching that was constantly taught throughout the entire tradition of the Church.[12] Moreover, according to the Holy Office the teaching was part of divine positive law and natural law which does not allow for an exception to the rule.

Why did the Holy Office and the entire moral tradition hold this? If an analysis of the moral act is given, we see that the act again violates the principle of the integral good specifically due to the circumstance of *By What Aid* (*Quibus Auxiliis*). The joining of prayers with others is normally a good thing, as rightly ordered praying is a morally good object. The intention may be good as well, such as trying to pray to end abortion or for peace during wartime. However, one is joining one's prayers to someone who is, on the objective order, standing outside the Catholic Church to which the elements of sanctification are entrusted. Since we are not permitted to judge the interior state of a person as to his or her faith, we are relegated to the exterior, i.e. the objective, order. That being the case, if a person is refusing to come into the Catholic Church which is the Church that Christ established (more on this later), one is, on the objective order, refusing a command from God of the natural law to obey Him in all things, part of which is His revelation. If a person refuses to come into the Catholic Church, he is either doing so because he denies the Catholic faith or, if he sees the truth of it, he refuses to submit to God and enter. So when a person prays with another person who is outside the

---

[10]This citation and many others are found in: Allen, "The Holy Office on Worship with Non-Catholics from 1622 to 1939."

[11]The terms *communicatio in sacris* and *communicatio in divinis* are often used by theologians interchangeably.

[12]A reading of the Fathers and Scholastic schools on the matter show unanimity on the matter which fulfills Pius IX requirements for a teaching to be of the faith (*de fide*); see *Tuas Libenter*, Denz. 2879/1683. See also Gregory IX, *Ab Aegyptiis* (Denz. 824/442) and Sixtus IV, *Romani Pontificis provida* (Denz. 1407).

Church, objectively speaking, he is joining his prayers with someone who manifests by his exterior action a refusal to accept what God has taught or to submit to what He has taught. That joining of the prayers to another person with that objective quality violates the principle of the integral good that one's actions be good in all of its aspects. Why did the application of this teaching change in the life of the Church? We shall address that in a subsequent chapter, but first we need to address another area of morality in which the principle of the integral good is often denied.

Chapter 3: Beauty, Movies and Music

When we think of entertainment in the modern context, we are struck by several things, chief among which is the artistic perfection with which some movies are produced. Our common experience of some movies is their artistic ability and technical perfection in being able to produce very specific emotional responses in audiences. While it may be able to be legitimately argued that the artistic beauty of much of modern music has declined significantly from the height of classic music in the past centuries, the music industry has achieved a technical ability to produce music that also has the ability to elicit certain emotional responses. One is also struck with the fact that at a time when the music industry has reached this technical and artistic zenith, it also links those occurrences in the music and movies to an intellectual message which is often contrary to man's good. While this is not the topic of this chapter, one must wonder what it means when people say, "that was a good movie" or "this is a good song." For this reason, it is important to address that very topic in relation to the principle of the integral good.

I. Distinctions of the Goods.

Before applying the principle of the integral good to movies and music, a distinction of goods must first be addressed. The scholastics, drawing from Aristotle[1], make a distinction between the useful good, the

---

[1] *Nicomachean Ethics*, l. VIII.

pleasurable good and the honest good.² The useful good (*bonum utile*) is that good which by its nature is ordered toward another good. For example, food is a useful good because it is ordered towards man's (and other animal's) health and sustenance. While we can give a consideration of food for its own sake, it specifically has to leave out the fact that food is fundamentally ordered towards the good of the one who eats it. Many things on this earth and in creation are that way, e.g. food, petroleum, the air we breathe, etc. Are movies and music useful goods? Yes, they can be. In fact, they are ordered toward man's use in some capacity, whether that is the eutrepalic³ or entertainment value (which is also part of the pleasurable good), the intellectual formation of others, etc. When analyzing art, in the strict sense, its primary function is not to be an expression of the artist, although that is part of it. In fact, art which seeks to merely be an expression of the artist and not a means of communication with others is disordered. This follows from the same reason as speech is not meant primarily so that the person talking can get the pleasure or satisfaction out of talking but as a means of communicating what we know or think to others. In like manner, art is a form of communication,⁴ in which the thoughts, aspirations, desires and inspirations of the artist draw the observer into the same thoughts, aspirations, etc. of the artist.⁵ This does not deny the reality that art is a form of self-expression, for this is based on the principle that the cause (artist) is always someway in the effect (art).⁶ However, that is not its principal function.

The second kind of good is the pleasurable good. Pleasure is not

---

²See II Sent., d. 21, q. 1, a. 3 and ST I, q. 5, a. 6 as examples in the works of St. Thomas.

³The virtue of eutrepelia is the virtue of right recreation which seeks to moderate the pleasures of play of which entertainment is part, both in kind and by degree or amount of use. St. Thomas considers it a subvirtue to modesty, see ST II-II, q. 160, a. 2.

⁴Any cursory search on the internet provides examples of this.

⁵This is why an artist who is morally disordered or who is not sane may be able to produce art that possesses excellence in expression but which the man of average virtue finds discordant and repugnant.

⁶SSP, p. 97, no. 95f.

something that can be sought for its own sake.[7] Rather pleasure, as Aristotle astutely described, is instantaneous, differs from motion, is complete and whole, accompanies motion, admits of degrees, occurs when there is a well-conditioned faculty to a fine or good object, varies based on faculty and condition, completes the activity, is a supervening good or end, and intensifies activity.[8] That entire description indicates that pleasure revolves around a faculty in relation to the object of the faculty. In other words, it is really about the faculty achieving its end in relation to the object rather than about the pleasure itself. So pleasure is not to be sought for its own sake when we analyze its nature, but rather the object which the faculty is ordered is sought for its own sake with the pleasure enhancing that process.

Is art, of which movies and music are a part, a pleasurable good? Indubitably, as we shall see later. But the pleasure itself is not what the art should be about. Rather, it should be about using the pleasure we get from art for the sake of virtue, knowledge, etc.

The honest good is that good which is sought for its own sake and to which other goods are ordered. So health is an honest good since food is ordered toward health. Sometimes one honest good is likewise the proximate good ordered even toward a remote good, i.e. one good ordered toward another. Even though we ought to order what we eat towards our health, in the end, the health is ordered toward our moral good, i.e. toward virtue, knowledge, the good of reason, etc. If the process becomes inverted, i.e. if we order the good of reason toward the good of food, pleasures, etc. and not toward the good of reason which is consummate with knowledge and the moral good which is recognized by reason, we are left bereft of right order.

II. Convertibility of the Beautiful with the Good

When we think of art, we naturally think of beauty since, normally speaking, it is the common experience of men that beautiful art is good art and good art is beautiful art. The relation of the beautiful to

---

[7] The history of philosophy is replete with discussions of this fact, but see ST I-II, q. 2, a. 6. The very fact that a vast majority of the philosophical tradition pointed out the flaws and limitations of the hedonistic philosophies is itself a testimony to this fact.

[8] Aristotle, *Nicomachean Ethics*, l. X.

the good centers around the fact that the good and the beautiful are convertible. Called transcendentals[9], being, the one, the good and the beautiful are all the same when we look at being itself except for the perspective we take on the being. That is to say, one can look at anything that exists and see it is good or beautiful when looked at from a specific perspective (*ratio* in Latin).

> The beautiful and the good in the subject, indeed, are the same, since they are founded upon the same thing, viz. upon form, and because of this, the good is praised as beautiful. But they differ in notion. For the good properly considers appetite, for that which is good is that which all things desire. And therefore, it has the notion of the end, for the appetite is as if a certain motion to the thing. Beauty, however, is with respect to a cognitive power, for the beautiful is that which once seen, it gives pleasure. Hence, beauty consists in due proportion, since the sense delights in things of due proportion, as in similar things to it; for also the sense is a certain perspective, as is also every cognitive power. And since knowledge occurs by assimilation, the similitude moreover with respect to form, beauty properly pertains to the notion of a formal cause.[10]

The beautiful and the good are being looked at from two different perspectives. The good is looked at from the point of view of appetite, i.e. something which is desired in order to fulfill the appetite in some way. So our appetite for food desires the good of the food for our fulfillment in

---

[9] See below for a fuller discussion of transcendentals.

[10] ST I, q. 5, a. 4, ad 1: pulchrum et bonum in subiecto quidem sunt idem, quia super eandem rem fundantur, scilicet super formam, et propter hoc, bonum laudatur ut pulchrum. Sed ratione differunt. Nam bonum proprie respicit appetitum, est enim bonum quod omnia appetunt. et ideo habet rationem finis, Nam appetitus est quasi quidam motus ad rem. Pulchrum autem respicit vim cognoscitivam, pulchra enim dicuntur quae visa placent. Unde pulchrum in debita proportione consistit, quia sensus delectatur in rebus debite proportionatis, sicut in sibi similibus; nam et sensus ratio quaedam est, et omnis virtus cognoscitiva. Et quia cognitio fit per assimilationem, similitudo autem respicit formam, pulchrum proprie pertinet ad rationem causae formalis.

some way. Whereas the beautiful is looked at from the point of view of that which pleases a cognitive faculty, i.e. some faculty which has the ability to know something on some level, whether that is the senses or our intellect. When we consider something beautiful, it causes us a certain pleasure just in its consideration as to whether we obtain the thing or not, e.g. one can look at Michelangelo's Pieta and be able to simply take intellectual pleasure or delight in its beauty without ever desiring to take the statue home and own it. Since the good and the beautiful are convertible, that is the same thing looked at from different points of view, what applies to the good also applies to the beautiful regarding the principle of the integral good. From this we see the necessity of talking about what, then, is truly beautiful.

III. The Attributes of Beauty

People state that what one holds as beautiful is merely a matter of personal preference or taste; "beauty is in the eye of the beholder." By reducing the discussion to merely one of subjective aesthetic sense or taste, they think they can keep at bay intellectual arguments about what they think is beautiful. However, a true analysis of beauty yields a very different conclusion. A basic look at beauty shows us that it has three attributes, viz. clarity, symmetry and completion or perfection.[11] Since these attributes of beauty constitute whether the *thing* is beautiful, something is objectively beautiful or it is not, if it possesses these attributes or not. The aesthetic sense, which we developed regarding those things that are beautiful, must therefore be in conformity with the beauty of the things as they are, since the aesthetic sense must be based on truth.

Truth is defined as the conformity of intellect and thing.[12] This means that one's ideas are true when they are in conformity with the way things are in reality. If a man thinks the grass outside is green when it is green, then his mind conforms to the things as they are and so he knows the truth about the grass. However, if he thinks that the grass is violet when it is really green, then he does not have the truth in his mind since his mind does not conform to reality. Aesthetic sense is the ability of the

---

[11] This section of the chapter is taken in large part from Ripperger, *Topics on Tradition*, chpt. 11.

[12] For a full discussion of the nature of truth, see De Ver., passim. Cf. Ripperger, *Introduction to the Science of Mental Health*, vol. 1, chpt. 5.

intellect to grasp what is *truly* beautiful. Given the aforesaid, an aesthetic sense is either true or false; one either finds pleasing that which is truly beautiful by having a true aesthetic sense or he finds things that are not truly beautiful as pleasing and thereby has a false aesthetic sense. In other words, beauty is not in the eye of the beholder, as commonly understood, but is objective, i.e. in the thing that is beautiful.

So what is art? St. Thomas Aquinas says that "art is nothing other than right reason of some produced works."[13] In other words, art is the application of right reason toward producing some kind of work. There are different kinds of work and so there are different kinds of art.

> While *mechanical* arts aim at the production of things useful, the *fine* arts aim at the production of something beautiful, i.e. of works which by their order, symmetry, harmony, splendor, etc., will give apt expression to human ideals of natural beauty as to elicit aesthetic enjoyment in the highest possible degree.[14]

The mechanical arts are there to produce things which we can use for the sake of our physical and spiritual benefit, such as cars, modern kitchen appliances, computers, etc. Here we see that technology is a branch of the mechanical arts.

The fine arts, on the other hand, are there to give expression to the beauty of the natural order which we see around us. This comes from Aristotle's observation that "art is the imitation of nature." It is a fact that any art whatsoever is always in some way imitative of nature. For even the most creative of artists take things which they have experienced and use them in different ways to express some idea or image which they have in their minds. For in order for us to have anything in the imagination, it must in some way come from what we sense in reality. Even in those works of art which seem to have nothing in common with reality, the artist takes colors and shapes which he gets from real things and fashions them according to his concept or idea. Nothing is in our imagination that was not first in the senses and so art has a connection to reality which is

---

[13] ST I-II, q. 57, a. 3: ars nihil aliud est quam ratio recta aliquorum operum faciendorum.

[14] Coffey, *Ontology or the Theory of Being*, p. 204.

not able to be denied.[15]

We therefore ask ourselves this question: if art is the imitation of nature, how are we to imitate it? Is good art merely a replication of some real thing? Is good art merely the art which expresses most clearly the conception of the artist? What if the artist is morally depraved and so his mode of thinking tends to distort everything according to his bad character?[16] In order to address this, we must delve deeper into what beauty is.

There are a number of definitions of beauty; many of them are true since they express different aspects of beauty. However, the best definition of beauty, in this author's opinion, is somewhat what we see above and is that used by St. Thomas Aquinas, viz. "beauty is that which is pleasing to a cognitive faculty."[17] Sometimes St. Thomas says it is that which is pleasing to sight (*visa*) but sight is of different kinds. There is physical sight which is a type of sense knowledge and there is intellectual sight and so we may say that beauty is that which pleases something which has the capacity to know. To demonstrate the truth of this definition, let us consider the following example: most women desire to be beautiful in order to please their husband or fiancé and that is why at their wedding women dress in a fashion to accentuate their beauty in such a way as to appear acceptable and pleasing so that he will say "I do" at the altar rail. No normal person wants to be ugly and this is natural to all of us: we desire to be beautiful in order to be pleasing to ourselves and others.

While all agree that we want to be beautiful, very few can agree on what is beautiful and for that reason, we must take a look at what the attributes of beauty are so that we can identify them in art. Beauty is a

---

[15] This does not mean that what the artist produces is merely a reproduction of some physical thing he sees before him at the moment but that his art takes from nature those elements which contain the beautiful and puts them together in the art, e.g. a man might paint a picture of a mountain which is beautiful, even though that mountain does not exist anywhere. Nevertheless, what is beautiful about a mountain is what is contained or manifest in mountains in nature.

[16] This question was dealt at length in E. Michael Jones' two works *Living Machines* and *Dionysos Rising*.

[17] See ST I-II, q. 27, a. 1, ad 3 ("pulchrum autem dicatur id cuius ipsa apprehensio placet") and Coffey, op. cit., p. 193.

transcendental and, as was observed, a transcendental is something that can be said of everything that exists. Metaphysicians do not always agree regarding the number of transcendentals, so we will only concern ourselves with a few. We can say that of all things that exist, everything that exists is a being, i.e. it is something which has existence. Everything that exists is also one and by this we understand that everything that is exists as an individual. We are distinct from each other and that is because we are separate beings. Everything that exists is good and this is because God created it and since everything that God creates reflects some perfection in God, then everything that exists is good since God is all good. We say that something is bad because it lacks some good or perfection and so we can say that insofar as something lacks being, it is evil.

If there is something lacking which should be in the thing, it is bad as we have seen with the entire discussion of the principle of the integral good and this is also applicable to beauty, insofar as if there is something lacking in something that should be there, it is not beautiful. In fact, something is ugly because it lacks beauty. For example, we would say that a person who has one eye that is significantly lower on his face than another or whose nose is bent to one side is ugly. This is because the person's face lacks symmetry which is one of the attributes of beauty.

In fact, there are three categories of attributes which a thing must possess in order for it to be beautiful. The first being *symmetry*, which is an attribute in things in which two or more parts are well arranged according to a proper order. It is sometimes called proportion and, in music, it is called harmony. The second attribute is *integrity*, sometimes called *perfection*. Integrity or perfection means that the thing is whole; that there are no parts of it missing that should be there. For example, if we see a person who is missing part of his face, we say the person is ugly, whereas the person, who has all of the parts of his face, assuming he has the other attributes of beauty, is beautiful. The third attribute of beauty is *clarity* or *splendor*. This attribute is present when something is beautiful and is thereby easily known or makes itself known. We can see this when we are in a crowd of people that someone who is very beautiful tends to naturally draw our attention. Aristotle used to call this amplitude insofar as a thing had be of a certain size in order to make itself easily known. Things that are too small are hard for us to know.

The reason we have made these distinctions is to point out that beauty is in the *thing*. In other words, beauty is the existence of these three attributes in the thing. All know the dictum "beauty is in the eye of the beholder," but the common understanding of this phrase is actually false. For we have just seen that beauty is something in the thing itself, for something is beautiful because in *it* are symmetry, proportion, clarity, etc. Let us do a short test to see if beauty is in the thing and not in the eye of the beholder: imagine if men who are married told their wives that they are not *really* beautiful. Each husband should tell his wife that beauty is in the eye of the beholder and so it is merely in his mind, not actually in her. If beauty is in the eye of beholder, women ought to forget doing all those things which accentuate their beauty and just find men who think they are beautiful. No. The fact is that beauty is in the thing and so the husbands can reassure their wives that they are beautiful, provided they really are.

  The problem is that people do not distinguish between beauty which is in the thing and the aesthetic sense which is in the person beholding the beauty. The aesthetic sense consists in the person's ability to grasp what is truly beautiful. Some people, as Aristotle says, are depraved and this affects their ability to see what is truly beautiful. There are several things which affect our ability to see what is beautiful. The first is our disposition; if we are in an angry mood, what we think is beautiful may be different from when we are in a good mood. We see disposition playing a role in that some people are naturally more attracted to people who are blond haired than to people who are black haired. Another thing that can affect what one thinks is beautiful is one's virtue. For certain virtues temper our appetites which have a capacity to affect our intellectual judgment. We often see people who are angry doing things they would not do outside that moment of anger and so the passion of anger tends to affect their judgement. Now beauty is something which we grasp or understand intellectually, so if our passions are disordered, it will affect our ability to judge whether something is really beautiful or not. This is why a good character in an artist is absolutely critical for him to be able to produce truly beautiful art. The last thing that we will discuss regarding those things which affect our aesthetic sense is our mental habits. If we are prone to error and we are habituated to think erroneously, our judgment about what is truly beautiful will be affected. This is why mental hygiene is important for grasping what is beautiful. Many of us have watched movies where the mentally disturbed villain observes that something is beautiful when in fact it is grotesque. It is here that we can also say that the more mentally ill the members of a society become, the more they are prone to error. The more they are prone to disordered passions in the living of their lives, the more will their art become grotesque.

Another attribute of beauty is that it naturally draws one to contemplation. Whenever we see something really beautiful, it naturally draws our intellect into considering it. For example, take the average male. If a beautiful woman walks into a room full of men, the men will follow her around the room with their eyes. If an ugly woman walks into the room, they will tend to keep doing what they are doing, i.e. she goes practically unnoticed. The point is that beauty naturally draws us to consider the thing which is beautiful. This is also why we can sit for a long period of time looking at a sunset or a view of a range of mountains. On the other hand, we tend to ignore or be repulsed by things that are really ugly.

Therefore, if art is truly beautiful, it will naturally draw people to contemplate that which is extolled by the art and this is true of movies and music. The beauty of the art will draw them to contemplate the art and the theme provides the subject matter of contemplation. The fact is that people are moved by what comes into the senses. If we present people with art that lacks clarity, proportion and symmetry and then we wonder why people are not interested in it, we only have ourselves to blame. We must conclude that the aesthetic sense of those who are uglifying the arts do not have the same habits of mind that we do. In fact, we dare say that they do not believe, think or grasp reality the same way we do. Art is, again, right reason applied to certain produced things. If someone does not have right reason, he will not have the right art. There is an intrinsic connection between right belief or thinking and beauty. When art is ugly and is held up as good art, it distorts a proper view of reality.

Can a person who is morally degenerate produce beautiful art? Potentially yes, but here we use the term *potential* because it is possible for someone who is morally degenerate to produce beautiful art. Yet, this is because there is something else compensating for his lack of good character. For instance, we cannot deny that there are some who can produce truly beautiful art, e.g. Mozart. But in these cases one cannot deny, or so it appears, that God has given them a particular gift or genius (not given to most) and so what may normally come through intellectual and moral virtues in some artists actually is able to be compensated for by the genius given to them by God. But let us not forget the principle that the cause is always some way in the effect. Unless there is something barring the artist's disorders from entering the art he produces, even if it is beautiful in some way, there will always be something "off" in the art he produces. The problem today is that many artists think they are a "genius" (but really are not) and have no virtue and it shows in their art.

Since the onslaught of modern philosophy, there has been a tendency to divorce man from reality. It is a fact that man comes to true intellectual knowledge of things by means of the senses. This means that what one puts in reality before men will often determine what they think; this is nowhere more clear than in the formative effect on culture by movies and music. While men have free will and so they can choose to reject what they see in reality, for either good or ill, nevertheless, most men are formed, both when they are young and when they are old, by what they see day to day. As modern philosophy divorced people from reality, people have begun thinking things which are contrary to reality. Many people's way of thinking has become detached from reality and has led to art suffering from several defects. The first is that art has become abstract. Our architecture and art are no longer based on what we find in reality but on abstract forms and shapes. Instead of having a building made of natural materials adorned with beauty, imitating things which we see, we are now seeing buildings made of glass and metals in abstract shapes and forms. Again, mental habits affect our aesthetic sense. As man began laboring under bad ideas, he formed habits which resulted in his art becoming ugly and yet he thinks it is beautiful. Modern architecture no longer has clarity as just mentioned; there is no proportion anymore; there is no symmetry. In fact, art and architecture today seem to be hallmarked by their disproportion and dissymmetry: the more of it the better, or so it seems.

This is a problem with modern society. The abstract way of thinking and the constant manipulation of created things have now intellectually formed two or three generations and is currently forming another generation because most of what the new generation sees is abstract architecture and art. The younger children are not having their imaginations filled with beauty and so they are less pleased and there is less joy. The irony of it is that while we are not filling our senses or the senses of our children with beautiful art which naturally draws us to intellectual considerations, we are leading lives which are immersed in sensuality.

On the societal level, if we want our culture(s) to be healthy and vibrant, there are two things, among others, which we must do. The first is we must propagate rightly ordered thinking so that others will be formed by it. The second is that we must erect art that inspires and draws people to contemplation. We can erect beautiful statues along highways and in the streets. We can build buildings that manifest true beauty, etc. The moral of the story is that we can begin transforming our culture by inundating the senses of the members of the society with art that is truly beautiful.

IV. Movies[18]

When we apply the above regarding art and beauty, we see that a movie has to be analyzed under different aspects to determine if the movie is truly good and by truly good we mean that it is an honest good. A movie by its technical prowess and some elements of beauty can sway people's emotions, but that is not the final end of the movie. It is a legitimate means and ought to be employed in order to bring people to the truth, but it is the truth, which is the good of the intellect,[19] and virtue which are the true honest goods of any real art. From this, we recognize that the principle of the integral good applies to the various goods of a movie. A movie can be integrally good from an artistic level, i.e. from the level of the natural good and therefore cause the pleasurable good. It can even be useful in different ways, but it is not truly useful unless it serves, or at least does not vitiate against, the full good of man, i.e. it does not go contrary to the honest good. For this reason, a movie can be artistically good in many elements but be morally bad. We say "many elements" because a movie which contains morally bad elements (more on that later) is not good artistically in *all* of its elements and therefore lacks true or complete beauty. In other words, to allow a script or a movie to contain morally bad elements already vitiates the beauty of the movie or script as well as its true artistic perfection.

When people say about a particular movie, "it was a good movie," one is often left with a few questions. Is it good because artistically it caused pleasure, e.g. the person says it is a good movie because the scenes were shot in iconically beautiful places or is good because the morals of the movie fulfilled the principle of the integral good? Is it good because the technical aspects of the movie were well executed but evil was glorified in the movie? Did it manipulate emotions well and that is why

---

[18]Under this topic of movies should include not just movies, but film, video, etc.

[19]For a discussion of this, see Ripperger, *Introduction to the Science of Mental Health*, vol. I, chpt. 5.

it is called a good movie while confirming people through the manipulations of the emotions to sympathize with people who commit crimes or gravely depraved acts?

Here we must make a distinction between what may be called simulatable acts and non-simulatable acts. Certain kinds of bad moral behavior can be simulated in such a manner that one is not truly doing the bad act, e.g. killing a man. We see that killing a person can be faked on stage or screen. No one of sound mind would assert that a movie or play was a "good" movie or play if they actually killed the person in real life on the stage or the screen. However, no one of sound mind would likewise assert that a particular scene in a movie was bad because the actor simulated the killing of a person in order to demonstrate some evil as truly bad. Examples of morally bad behavior that can be simulated would include but not be limited to: killing, lying, stealing, acts of fraud, etc.

Simulatable acts are counter distinguished from non-simulatable acts in that non-simulatable acts are morally bad because by their nature they cannot be faked. For example, immodesty on screen is still immodest insofar as the man of average virtue, to protect his interior moral state, cannot look at the scene without allowing disordering affections in his mind and heart. Using our Lord's name in vain (called profanity) or certain base terms (called vulgarity) also cannot be used without detracting from the moral good of the movie. Since the only way we do not use Our Lord's name in vain is to use it demonstrably[20] or in devotion, such as prayer, then any use of it outside that context is offensive to God and right morals. Another example might make this clear. If a married man received a video of his wife which was highly entertaining but quite offensive to her because it made her look evil, the husband would offend his wife by playing and laughing at the video. Each time he did it, she would take offense by it and it is not enough that he does not play the video but still keeps it because it is funny. The very fact that he would continue to own it or keep it would offend her. The same applies to good morals in relation to non-simulatable acts in movies.

Some argue that it would then be impossible to make real life movies of things such as war where the soldiers often use all sorts of profanity and vulgarity or scenes where a couple argues, etc. This is simply not true when we view the history of movies in these areas. Part

---

[20] For example, if one were to say: "God is all good," such use is a demonstrable use of His Name and does not offend Him as it is a true statement said in a proper context.

of artistic genius is the ability to portray things which are horrific, the sufferings of those involved and the evils people endured without the need to resort to non-simulatable acts.

Lastly, while simulatable acts are not in themselves morally bad when employed in a movie, some simulatable acts can adversely affect the virtue and mental health of the audience; for example, having battle scenes that scar the imagination for long periods of time. Artists must realize that to fulfill the principle of the integral good, they must keep a proper perspective on what they produce and its effect, morally, psychologically as well as artistically, in relation to the audience.

V. Music

St. Thomas observes that "musical instruments move the soul more to pleasure (delight) rather than form a good interior disposition."[21] This indicates two things. The first is that music does not form a good disposition. By this it would appear that St. Thomas means that the principal effect of music is not to cause a dispositional change in the person. Although we do say that music soothes the savage beast which can mean that when one is disposed one way (e.g. to anger), it is possible to dispose the person in another way (e.g. towards the passion of love) through the pleasure of music. Today, with the capabilities of high powered amplification, music can be used to cause physiological changes in the body by the power of the vibrations acting upon the body. These vibrations can also cause pleasure independently of the auditory aspect of music. The second aspect of this quote is that music causes pleasure. Since music is something auditory, i.e. sensory, it enters into the imagination and causes pleasure. This pleasure may be of two kinds. The first is appetitive, insofar as the music moves the sensitive appetites.[22] Different kinds of music tend to elicit different kinds of appetites. Some music moves the concupiscible appetite to love, as when we see that some music moves people to be more amorous. Some music moves the irascible

---

[21] ST II-II, q. 91, a. 2, ad 4: "musica instrumenta magis animum movent ad delectationem quam per ea formetur interius bona dispositio." This section of the chapter is taken in substance from, Ripperger, *Introduction to the Science of Mental Health*, vol. III, chpt. 2.

[22] *In Psalmos*, p. 32,n. 2: "item consonantiae musicae immutant hominis affectum."

appetite, e.g. certain forms of military music incite the soldiers to fight harder. Horror movies make use of certain kinds of instruments and music to elicit the passion of fear in the audience. In fact, the modern movie industry is a testimony to the profound grasp man has of the ability of music to elicit any kind of passion. This artistic ability is a particularly strong psychological force when it accompanies the right kinds of images.[23]

Because music enters the imagination, it has the ability to affect not just the appetites but the power of association in our minds as well, particularly when the music evokes an emotional or appetitive reaction. As the person experiences the passion evoked by the music, the person associates that form of music with the pleasure of the passion. Hence, when someone listens to music often, he becomes habituated to assessing the music in a positive fashion due to the pleasure. This positive assessment is then merged with the image and thereby affects the judgement of the intellect. It is for this reason that people will often say that a particular form of music is "good," even though it can be morally degenerate. If the music is listened to enough and if it is disordered but still gives pleasure, it is possible for the music to habituate the person according to vice. Music, since it can affect judgment, can also affect volition and here we see that music can have a direct impact on the moral life of the individual. Because it can affect the various psychological faculties, it has the ability to affect people's mental health and growth in virtue. In this sense, the use of music can cause (aid) mental health or destroy it.[24] When it is joined to disordered imagery, it is even more lethal.

Because music affects the emotions, teens and even adults can become attached to musical forms which elicit the emotions. For example, soft rock tends to affect the concupiscible emotions while hard rock or acid rock tends to elicit irascible emotions. Because of the instability of the emotional life of teens due to the dispositional changes in the body arising from puberty, for the sake of the virtue of teens, music to which

---

[23] Images can affect how we judge the music and the music can affect how we judge and appetitively react to a particular image.

[24] The use of music in psychological warfare indicates that when the music is played at a high volume with specific kinds of melodies, it can have a destabilizing effect on the listener, especially when he does not exercise control over the music. Essentially, this indicates that the music affects the imagination, which in turn affects his judgment and volition.

they listen should be regulated by their parents. When teens are allowed to listen to whatever form of music they want in the amount that they want, their virtue or lack thereof is affected thereby. This does not mean that they will be gravely affected, but they may.

Plato observes:

> But, as things are with us, music has given occasion to a general conceit of universal knowledge and contempt for law, and liberty has followed in their train. Fear was cast out by confidence in supposed knowledge, and the loss of it gave birth to impudence. For to be unconcerned for the judgment of one's betters in the assurance which comes of a reckless excess of liberty is nothing in the world but reprehensible impudence.[25]

Because music gives pleasure, if one gives oneself over to it without restraint, it tends to take on a life of its own. In other words, license regarding the pleasure of music leads to license in other areas of one's life. As a result, those who seek to restrict one's license are judged with contempt, e.g. those in authority and laws themselves. Parents will often find that a teenager who listens to music without restriction becomes difficult to handle and unruly. This is why Plato thought that music had to be regulated by the state, because it constituted such a powerful (psychological) force.

Implicit in this discussion is the fact that, since music has the ability to affect the appetites, it has the ability to corrupt the virtues of temperance and fortitude in an individual. If a person does not listen to rightly ordered music or does not moderate his listening to music and the pleasure taken therein, it can corrupt temperance and make him intemperate. Likewise, since fortitude is a virtue lying in a mean between the excess of rashness and the defect of cowardice,[26] music which moves the irascible appetite excessively can corrupt fortitude. In like manner, if one listens to music for the sake of pleasure and does so without restraint, he will become attached to the pleasure and be unwilling to engage the arduous good which requires pain. As a consequence, one may become cowardly. Based on this analysis, it can even be said that license in the

---

[25] Plato, *Laws III* (701a and b).

[26] ST II-II, q. 123, a. 3.

area of the pleasures of music can lead to effeminacy.[27] Effeminacy is a sorrow and an unwillingness to be separated from pleasure in order to pursue the arduous.[28] If males do not moderate the pleasures of music, they can become attached to them and thereby become effeminate.

Connected to the discussion of how music can corrupt virtues, we may say that music does not only have the capacity to corrupt temperance and fortitude but also prudence. This should be clear from the words of Plato above. However, since intemperance can affect one's judgment regarding what is prudent, if one is intemperate about the pleasures of music, this will lead to imprudence. Since prudence is an act of the possible intellect in which the universally known principles are applied in the concrete,[29] prudence requires rectitude of the image in the imagination by which the person is put into contact with the singular concrete circumstances. If intemperance affects the imagination, it will have the effect of drawing reason to excess and defect regarding its judgments. Therefore, prudence which requires coming to the knowledge of the mean in regard to actions will be corrupted by excesses in judgment.

If the pleasures of music can corrupt prudence, they can also corrupt the virtue of decorum. Decorum is the virtue by which one moderates one's externals.[30] Externals are of different kinds, including things such as dress, actions and possessions. Decorum is the virtue by which we moderate our dress in two ways. The first is to modesty[31] by which one takes due solicitude about not drawing others into sins of impurity. The second is more proper to decorum itself insofar as one's dress fits one's circumstances and one's state in life, e.g. decorum is the virtue which regulates doctors wearing a proper attire when practicing medicine or a priest wearing clerics when in public. But decorum also ensures that we do not go to excess in our dress, e.g. if a person were to wear very expensive clothing and jewelry to an informal dinner, his dress would not fit the circumstances. In this respect, the pleasure of music

---

[27] See Cole, *Music and Morals*, p. 25.

[28] See ST II-II, q. 138, a. 1.

[29] ST II-II, q. 47, a. 6.

[30] See ST II-II, q. 143, a. 1.

[31] See ST II-II, q. 168.

affects the judgment of the person and corrupts prudence regarding dress, i.e. it corrupts decorum by making him think certain kinds of dress, speech and comportment are good when they are not. This is why those in the rock music scene tend towards immodesty in dress. It is also why some of them tend toward the piercing of body parts which are not suited by their nature to being pierced, e.g. the tongue, and this is to say nothing regarding tattoos. It is why they tend to "make a statement" by their dress, piercings and tattoos. We also see the connection to Plato's observation that they will tend to reject authority and laws and their dress is often seen as a statement against the rules and customs of a society.

Decorum also moderates our external actions so that our actions fit the circumstances and our state in life. For instance, children who have not reached the age of reason and therefore are not yet capable of developing the virtues, tend to say things out of place which are often very embarrassing to the parents. In like manner, when one does not moderate the pleasures of music, it tends to affect one's exterior behavior. Since prudence is affected, the person will often judge based upon the pleasure of the moment rather than what right reason would dictate. Since a person can become habituated to judge according to pleasure by not moderating the pleasures of music, he will tend to act out according to the pleasures of the passions rather than according to reason. The manifestation of this problem is seen when teens and adults who listen to appetitive music without moderation tend to act erratically or irrationally. It is also manifest in their lack of reverence for elders, parents and authority figures in general. This is why there is a close connection between sex, drugs and rock and roll.[32] Each gives a form of pleasure and each constitutes something to which one can become addicted. While addiction to the pleasures of music may be more culturally acceptable, nevertheless it does exhibit a lack of the virtue of temperance.

While appetitive pleasure is the first kind of pleasure which is caused by music, the second kind of pleasure which music gives is intellective pleasure. Beauty is that which is pleasing to a cognitive faculty.[33] In this respect, if music is truly beautiful, it is pleasing to the

---

[32] Sometimes sex, drugs and rock and roll are done together at the same time in order for the person's experience of each to be enhanced.

[33] ST I-II, q. 27, a. 1, ad 3: "Ad vim cognoscitivam, ita quod bonum dicatur id quod simpliciter complacet appetitui; pulchrum autem dicatur id cuius ipsa apprehensio placet."

possible intellect. We must clearly distinguish between the pleasure that arises out of music which appeals to the sensitive appetites (emotions) and the pleasure which the intellect obtains in the consideration of the harmony, clarity and perfection of the music. Beauty also draws one to contemplation,[34] i.e. it tends to draw one toward an interior intellectual reflection.

If music is beautiful, it can enhance the intellectual activity to which it is joined. Therefore music which moves the intellect to a consideration of the thing to which the music is joined can aid study and learning. St. Thomas says in the *Summa Theologiae*:

> it is the same reason to the hearers, in which, although sometimes they may not understand what is sung, nevertheless they understand why (*propter quid*) it is sung, namely to the praise of God.[35]

A person may understand what is sung and the music enhances his understanding by joining music to the thing of consideration which provides more information about the thing considered. For example, if a person watches a sad scene in a movie, he knows it is something of sorrow, but when sorrowful music is joined to it, it increases his understanding of the evil or sorrow. Even if the person does not understand what is sung, e.g. a person may not understand the words of Latin in Gregorian chant, he can nevertheless recognize in the harmony and melody of the music, what the music is saying or how it is directing our consideration. For instance, the glory of God is reflected by a particular mode of Gregorian Chant or the seriousness of final judgment is reflected in the mode or tones of the *Dies Irae*. Conversely, if the music is too appetitive, i.e. it elicits emotions more than intellectual contemplation, or if the music lacks beauty,[36] it can detract from the consideration of the truth and from contemplation. Ugly music can

---

[34] Coffey, *Ontology*, p. 193ff.

[35] ST II-II, q. 91, a. 2, ad 5: "Et eadem est ratio de audientibus, in quibus, etsi aliquando non intelligant quae cantantur, intelligunt tamen propter quid cantantur, scilicet ad laudem Dei."

[36] While beautiful music can elicit emotions, generally speaking, it appears that music which lacks beauty tends to be more appetitive.

distract one from study and learning.[37]

Modern studies are discovering that the playing of music can contribute to learning. Playing music increases intelligence by stimulating certain parts of the brain.[38] Other studies are finding that musical training increases math ability, i.e. it increases the person's ability to engage in spatial-temporal reasoning.[39] The Scholastics held that the study of music is a subalternated science (and art) to mathematics,[40] so they knew that learning music has a connection to intellectual formation.

Since music can draw us to contemplation or move our emotions, it constitutes a force by which people can be directed. St. Thomas observes:

> the affections of man are directed by instrumental and harmonious music in three ways: sometimes it establishes a certain rectitude and strength of the soul; sometimes one is drawn up into the heights; sometimes into sweetness and delight.[41]

The soul of the person is directed by music in three ways. The first is that it tends to strengthen the soul and directs it in the right thing. Plato says

---

[37] Students are known to listen to appetitive forms of music while studying. This is often done to provide appetitive pleasure to the arduous task of studying. However, the pleasures of the music are not ordered toward the things studied and therefore tend to distract more than enhance studying.

[38] Jim Wilson, *Cognitive Chords*, as found on 10/1/03 on the website of *Popular Mechanics* at http://www.popularmechanics.com/science/research/2002/3/cognitive_chords/index.phtml.

[39] *fMRI Study of Correlation between Musical Training and Math Ability*, as found on 10/1/03 at http://www.irc.chmcc.org/Research_Areas/brain/fMRI/musicmathcorr.htm.

[40] See *In libros physicorum*, l. 1, c. 2, n. 4.

[41] *In Psalmos*, p. 32, n. 2: Affectus enim hominis per instrumenta et consonantias musicas dirigitur, quantum ad tria: quia quandoque instituitur in quodam rectitudine et animi firmitate: quandoque rapitur in celsitudinem: quandoque in dulcedinem et jucunditatem. See also ST II-II, q. 91, a. 2.

that the purpose of music is to take pleasure and pain in the right things.[42] Since music can affect judgment, it is clear that music can be used to direct people to the truth and to judge things rightly, not only in the speculative order but also in the practical order. Music can be used to move people to judge prudently[43] and if it can affect prudence, music can be used to develop virtue by moving people to perform acts of virtue. It is for this reason that Aristotle says that music forms character.[44] This forming of character can be done by directing the appetitive life of people to virtue. Music can also be used to portray character,[45] e.g. when we see a stern and evil man portrayed by low menacing tones. This also contributes to the building of character since people can be drawn to judge based upon virtue and vice rather than on the mere pleasure of the music.

Plato even says that music can be used to represent the masculine and the feminine.[46] If music is joined to the right kinds of imagery, it is possible for the music to directly contribute to the mental distinctions that people make about masculine and feminine character, both as to what is unsuited to those characters and what is suited to them.

> It will further be necessary to make a rough general distinction between two types of songs, those suited for females and those suited for males, and so we shall have to provide both with their appropriate scales and rhythms. ... Now it is perfectly possible to make the necessary regulations for both kinds of songs in both respects, but natural distinction of sex, which should therefore be our basis for discrimination. Accordingly, we shall pronounce the majestic and whatever tends to valor masculine, while it will be the tradition of our law

---

[42] Plato, *Laws II* (659d).

[43] In Job, c. 21.

[44] Aristotle, *Politics*, l. VIII, chap. 5 (1339a12-1340b19). We can say not only does it form character in a positive sense but as was seen above it can also form character in a negative sense.

[45] Aristotle, *Poetics*, chap. 1 (1447a27).

[46] Plato, *Laws II* (669c).

> and our theory alike that what makes rather for order and purity is peculiarly feminine.[47]

Since masculinity and femininity are accentuated by the stressing of different traits, music can contribute to the forming of masculine and feminine character. Previously, it was noted that listening to music without moderation regarding the pleasures of the music can lead to effeminacy. We see that this is the case with men. If men are forced to embrace or listen to forms of music which are more active on the concupiscible appetite than the irascible appetite and the intellect, it will have a feminizing effect on them. Not that they can never listen to such forms, but their listening must be more moderated and directed intellectually, so as not to have a feminizing effect on the men. Conversely, women who tend to listen to masculine music too much may take on characteristics proper only to men. Again, not that we cannot listen to music which affects the irascible appetite, but that we must be moderate listening to those forms of music and intellectually direct the appetites while doing so. Given normal, virtuous women and men, they will tend toward those forms of music in congruity with dispositions of their gender.

Yet, it should not be assumed that music is unmanly. Since it can form character by forming virtue, music can be manly. Virtue tends to temper the soul and moderate it, both with women and men. Plato observes that, if one never listens to music, it makes one hard and savage and yet, if one listens to music too much, it can make one soft and gentle.[48] The pleasures of music can have a tempering effect, not only on men but on women. Yet, due sollicitude must be taken to ensure that the pleasures of music neither make men effeminate nor cause lack of temperance in women.

We can begin to see why Plato said that it is false that the standard for good music is whether it causes pleasure.[49] Rather, music, which is part of the divine providential plan, is ordered toward the good of the soul, i.e. towards rectitude and strength of soul (virtue). The criteria for good music and bad music cannot be based purely upon the

---

[47] Plato, *Laws VII* (802e).

[48] Plato, *Republic III* (410c).

[49] Plato, *Laws II* (655d).

fact that a particular form causes pleasure. Such a position is nothing short of hedonism. Rather, good and bad music must be judged based on two distinct criteria. The first is its artistic merit (the natural good), i.e. some music is more beautiful than others and some music is more capable of directing the appetitive life than others. The second is the moral character (the moral good): those forms of music which tend to erode moral virtue, either because of their lyrics or because of their melody and musical quality, constitute a danger to people's well being and their psychological health. Those forms of music which tend to build moral virtue are good insofar as their lyrics and musical style promote what is noble in man and in God's creation. It is possible to have morally bad lyrics with morally good harmony and vice versa. However, such music is inherently disordered.

The second way in which music directs the soul, according to St. Thomas, is that it draws one up into the heights. By this, St. Thomas means that it tends to lift the soul to the consideration of those things which are above him. In this respect, music can lift the soul away from earthly things to heaven as well as to that which is most noble in man.[50] Music can be used to incite man to God[51] and so music can aid man's happiness by helping him advance towards his final end. On the other hand, we may say that music which tends to appetitive disorder detracts one from the final end and results in the person and society imbued with that form of music being drawn towards unhappiness, lack of peace (strife) and disorder.

The third way that music directs the soul is by sweetness and delight. This has already been seen with respect to the intellectual and appetitive pleasure given by music. Since music affects the various faculties of the soul, it has an ability to cause spiritual joy (by lifting one's mind and heart to the Object of joy which is God) and delight of the soul (by seeing the goodness of God as reflected in the perfections of the harmony of the music).[52]

---

[50] *In Psalmos*, p. 32, n. 2 and ST II-II, q. 91, a. 2. Given this, it would seem that certain kinds of music can contribute to the gift of the Holy Ghost of Fear of the Lord and even to Wisdom by disposing the soul to these gifts.

[51] *In Psalmos*, p. 32, n. 2.

[52] Pius XII, *Musicae Sacrae*, par. 4. Which forms of music finds themselves in religious ritual must not be based upon the pleasure it gives the congregation but upon whether it lifts the minds and souls of the congregation to God. It is very easy for

Given all of this, we can see that in order for music to fulfill the principle of the integral good, two things must be in place. The first is that the music must be truly beautiful. The attempts by artists to switch the scales of music from diatonic to chromatic forms of music did not aid the beauty of music since the diatonic forms represent what is present in nature as to natural tones whereas chromatic music was an intentional departure from art imitating nature. Does this mean that one cannot use different forms in music itself or in movies? Not necessarily. If forms of music which are dissonant (chromatic) in order to associate in the song or in the movie something that is evil, then it can have a right order, but it ought not be the predominate aspect of the song unless the song is to portray evil discussed throughout the song as truly evil or in the movies portraying the evil as truly evil. But since our focus ought to be the good and not evil, as a general rule, for the sake of our psychological and moral well being, the music should not be predominately dissonant and the same applies to music. The second thing that needs to be in place is that the lyrics ought to be rightly ordered, not just morally but also psychologically to fulfill the principle of the integral good. One of the unfortunate occurrences in our culture is the tendency to link beautiful music with disordered lyrics and that is to say nothing about promoting entire forms of music that always tend to man's disorder. Lyrics (music we may even say in general) are ordered towards man's formation, as we saw above. It is not enough for a person to assert that a form of music is "good" when it is morally bad or has a deleterious effect on the average man's moral life. To do so lacks making the proper distinctions and is a sign of shallow thinking.

Nor can the sole responsibility for viewing bad movies and listening to bad music be laid at the feet of those who produce them. While it is true that someone who produces a movie or music which contains something morally bad offends God each time it is played and each time it appears on the screen, the fact is that people can cooperate in another person's sins in a variety of ways. In the case of movies and music, each time someone presses the play button knowing that the movie contains a moral evil that is non-simulatable, he is responsible for that moral evil in God's creation which was created for His glory. Each time he does so, he detracts from the glory of God in the created order is detracted from.

---

musicians who are not properly refined or educated to assume that eliciting emotions from people is the same as causing a "religious experience."

Chapter 4: Ecclesiology

I. A Short History of a Problem

William Palmer, an Oxford theologian, was the principal originator of what is called the "Branch Theory." His two-volume *Treatise on the Church of Christ*, written in 1838 gave written expression to the idea. As it began to spread with mixed acceptance, Catholic theologians began to address it. The theory essentially states that

> though the Church may have fallen into schism within itself and its several provinces or groups of provinces be out of communion with each other, each may yet be a branch of the one Church of Christ, provided that it continues to hold the faith of the original undivided Church and to maintain the Apostolic Succession of its bishops. Such, it is contended by many Anglican theologians, is the condition of the Church at the present time, there being now three main branches.

This is sometimes given a metaphysical analysis stating that there are varying degrees of participation in the one Church of Christ but that all these various churches, while not having the unity of government, are still part of the one Church which Christ established. This view allows for many different variations. While the branch theory tends to stick to apostolic succession as the source of being a branch in the true Church, later theologians would extend inclusion in the Church to a church or religion that believes in the Trinity and Incarnation.

II. The Ecclesiastical Response to the "Branch" Theory

A. The Response of Catholic Theologians

Almost immediately after the theory was proposed by the Anglicans, Catholic theologians addressed the topic rather thoroughly.[1] The OCE points out that this particular theory in relationship to ecclesiology is a novelty,[2] even though the Fathers of the Church and the medieval theologians addressed what constitutes unity with the Church which Christ established. What the theologians were consistent in pointing out is that ultimately the Anglican theory led to the destruction of the *visible* unity of the Church and substituted it for only an *invisible* unity.[3] It is from this theory that we begin to see the terminological change in relation to the expression *sister churches* in reference to those religions which are outside the communion of the holy Roman Catholic Church.[4] Historically, the term *sister church* only referred to those different rites within the Catholic Church.

The question became, what was the principle of unity or what is necessary for a particular community to be said to be in unity with the Church that Christ established. To that end, the theologians noted that it was based upon the unity of or the possession of the same faith, government and sacraments.[5] By *same* here is meant that they have the

---

[1] See, among others, Billot, *De Ecclesia Christi*, p. 150; Del Val, *The Truth of Papal Claims*, p. 127f; Guilbert, *De Christi Ecclesia*, p. 84f; Bainvel, *De Ecclesia Christi*, p. 51 and Berry, *The Church of Christ*, p. 39.

[2] Under the entry "Church", OCE discusses in relationship to the Branch Theory the fact that this is a novelty.

[3] For example, see Berry, *The Church of Christ*, p. 39.

[4] See Pesch, *Institutiones Propaedeuticae ad Sacram Theologiam*, Vol. I, p. 274.

[5] Billot, *De Ecclesia Christi*, p. 150; Guilbert, *De Christi Ecclesia*, p. 84f; Bainvel, *De Ecclesia Christi*, p. 51 and Berry, *The Church of Christ*, p. 39.

whole faith, the *whole* government and *all* the sacraments[6], thereby excluding schismatics. Within this context, two things emerge in relationship to this particular ecclesiological discussion: (1) that without the whole faith, and the whole government and all the sacraments, one is not part of the *true* Church[7] which Christ established and (2) the emergence of the papacy as *the* principle of unity.[8] Given these two, only the Roman Catholic Church and those in union with it can be said to be part of the Church that Christ established.[9]

B. The Response of the Magisterium

Soon after the formulation of the Branch Theory, the Holy Office, in a letter to the Bishops of England,[10] rejected the idea that "the three Christian communions, Roman Catholic, Greek schismatic, and Anglican, however separated and divided from one another, nevertheless with equal right claim for themselves the name Catholic" and "together now constitute the Catholic Church." However, it was necessary to address the topic more definitively.

During the First Vatican Council, the Council fathers defined the following propositions:

> In order, then, that the episcopal office should be one and undivided and that, by the union of the clergy, the whole multitude of believers should be held together in the unity of faith and communion, he set blessed Peter over the rest of the apostles and instituted in him the permanent principle of both unities and their visible

---

[6]Guilbert, *De Christi Ecclesia*, p. 84f and Bainvel, *De Ecclesia Christi*, p. 51, para. 4. Here we begin to see the connection to the principle of the integral good.

[7]See Billot, *De Ecclesia Christi*, p. 154; Pesch, loc. cit.

[8]This will ultimately be the Church's response as we shall see below. However Cardinal Merry Del Val (*The Truth of Papal Claims*, page 128) observes: "the Church is the mystical body of Christ, and where Peter is, there is the church, as the fathers said of old."

[9]Billot, *De Ecclesia Christi*, p. 154

[10] Denz. 2300/1685 (September 16th, 1864).

foundation.[11]

Several things are occurring in this passage. The first is that the papacy or the Petrine office is established as the permanent principle in relationship to the various forms of unity. The office of the papacy itself becomes *the* principle of unity while the others are principles of unity. To formulate this more clearly, it may be said that in order for one to be in union with the Church which Christ established, it is necessary to have unity in faith, unity in government, and unity in sacraments, etc. All of these are principles of unity so that each one is *a* principle of unity but not *the* principle of unity. It is not possible to be in union with the Church that Christ established, i.e. the Roman Catholic Church, without having each of these principles of unity in their entirety. However, having one of those without being united under the papacy in government, i.e. without being united to *the* principle of unity itself, i.e. the papacy, one is not in union with the Church that Christ established.

One finds in the schema that was proposed for the fathers of the First Vatican Council to consider the following Canon:

> If anyone were to say that the One True Church is not one body in itself but from various and separate Christian societies in name consisting and diffused through them or that the various societies differing from each other in the profession of faith and separate in communion as members or parts constitute the one and universal Church of Christ, anathema sit.[12]

This canon did not make it into the final document at the First Vatican

---

[11] Pastor Aeternus, para. 4: Ut vero episcopatus ipse unus et indivisus esset et per cohaerentes sibi invicem sacerdotes credentium multitudo universa in fidei et communionis unitate conservaretur beatum Petrum caeteris apostolis praeponens in ipso instituit perpetuum utriusque unitatis principium ac visibile fundamentum.

[12] *Concilium Vaticanum I: Schemata patrum examini proposita et capita addenda: Schema De Doctrina Catholica*, can IV: Si quis dixerit veram ecclesiam non esse unum in se corpus sed ex variis dissitisque christiani nominis societatibus constare per easque diffusam esse aut varias societates ab invicem fidei professione dissidentes atque communione seiunctas tanquam membra vel partes unam et universalem constituere Christi ecclesiam anathema sit.

Council. Due to the Franco-Prussian war, the First Vatican Council was cut short . The fathers of the Council completed the document *Pastor Aeternus* during the fourth session, but suspended the Council due to the war. When the schema including the anathema was published, it did contain an *imprimatur* in the text in which it is published, and it does express the general thought of the time, viz. that the Church was not constituted by a variety of different Christian societies which did not profess the same faith.

Shortly after the first Vatican Council, Pope Leo XIII in the document *Satis Cognitum* addresses the topic more thoroughly. He observes that the true Church which Christ established is one and that Christ did not intend to establish a church which embraced several similar communities which were distinct.[13] By this, Pope Leo XIII is rejecting the Branch Theory. He goes on to say:

> The Church alone offers to the human race that religion—that state of absolute perfection—which He wished, as it were, to be incorporated in it. And it alone supplies those means of salvation which accord with the ordinary counsels of Providence.[14]

Essentially, what Pope Leo XIII is saying is that there is only one Church and that this Church constitutes the only divinely established means of salvation and that to be part of this Church one must be "subject to one and the same authority"[15] i.e. the papacy. For this reason, those who fall away from the unity of the Church by schism as well as by heresy[16] are not part of that Church which Christ established nor can anyone who

---

[13] Para. 4.

[14] Para. 9: Ista igitur omnia inesse in Ecclesia oportet, quippe quae Servatoris munia in aevum persequitur: religionem, quam in ea velut incorporan ille voluit, mortalium generi omni ex parte absolutam sola praestat: itemque ea, quae ex ordinario providentiae consilio sunt instrumenta salutis, sola suppeditat. We shall prescind from the discussion of who constitutes an actual member of this Church as to individuals and the salvation of those outside the Church since that itself constitutes an entire chapter or book.

[15] Para 10: uni eidemque subiectus potestati.

[16] See para. 10.

dissents from the Roman faith be a Catholic.[17]

> From this it must be clearly understood that Bishops are deprived of the right and power of ruling, if they deliberately secede from Peter and his successors; because, by this secession, they are separated from the foundation on which the whole edifice must rest. ...When the Divine founder decreed that the Church should be one in faith, in government, and in communion, He chose Peter and his successors as the principle and center, as it were, of this unity.[18]

This last quote taken with what is above is very important because it addresses the question of the Orthodox religions which are in schism from the Roman Catholic Church. In effect, as we shall see more later, these religions cannot be said to participate in the Catholic Church merely because of the fact that they have material apostolic succession.

After Leo XIII, Pope Pius XI issued a document which likewise addressed certain issues in relationship to the question of unity with that Church which Christ established. In his document
Mortalium Animos, he observed:

> A good number of them, for example, deny that the Church of Christ must be visible and apparent, at least to such a degree that it appears as one body of faithful, agreeing in one and the same doctrine under one teaching authority and government; but, on the contrary, they understand a visible Church as nothing else than a Federation, composed of various communities of Christians, even though they adhere to different doctrines, which may even be incompatible one with

---

[17]Para. 13.

[18]Para 15: Ex quo plane intelligitur, excidere episcopos iure ac potestate regendi, si a Petro eiusve successoribus scientes secesserint. Nam a fundamento, quo totum debet aedificium niti, secessione divelluntur... Videlicet cum Ecclesiam divinus auctor fide et regimine et communione unam esse decrevisset, Petrum eiusque successores delegit in
quibus principium foret ac velut centrum unitatis.

another. Instead, Christ our Lord instituted His Church as a perfect society, external of its nature and perceptible to the senses, which should carry on in the future the work of the salvation of the human race, under the leadership of one head, with an authority teaching by word of mouth, and by the ministry of the sacraments, the fonts of heavenly grace; for which reason He attested by comparison the similarity of the Church to a kingdom, to a house, to a sheepfold, and to a flock.

They add that the Church in itself, or of its nature, is divided into sections; that is to say, that it is made up of several churches or distinct communities, which still remain separate, and although having certain articles of doctrine in common, nevertheless disagree concerning the remainder; that these all enjoy the same rights; and that the Church was one and unique from, at the most, the apostolic age until the first Ecumenical Councils.[19]

The various ideas enumerated here have become very widespread and have even been adopted by certain members of the Magisterium within the last 50 years. The point to draw out here is that many of the theories are still alive and well today regarding various degrees of participation in

---

[19]Para. 6f. Ex iis enim bene multi, exempli causa, negant, Ecclesiam Christi adspectabilem acque conspicuam esse oportere, eatenus saltem, quatenus unum apparere debeat fidelium corpus, in una eademque doctrina sub uno magisterio ae regimine concordium; at, contra, Ecclesiam adspectabilem seu visibilem intellegunt non aliud esse, nisi Foedus ex variis christianorum communitatibus compositum, licet aliis aliae doctrinis, vel inter se pugnantibus, adhaereant. Ecclesiam vero suam instituit Christus Dominus societatem perfectam, natura quidem externam obiectamque sensibus, quae humani generis reparandi opus, unius capitis ductu, per vivae vocis magisterium perque sacramentorum, caelestis gratiae fontium, dispensationem, in futurum tempus persequeretur; quamobrem et regno et domni et ovili et gregi eam comparando similem affirmavit.

Addunt, Ecclesiam per se, seu natura sua, in partes esse divisam, idest ex plurimis ecclesiis seu communitatibus peculiaribus constare, quae, disiunctae adhuc, etsi nonnulla doctrinae capita habent communia, tamen in reliquis discrepant; iisdem sane iuribus frui singulas; Ecclesiam, ad summum, ab aetate apostolica ad priora usque Oecumenica Concilia unicum atque unam fuisse.

one Church of Christ by those outside the Catholic Church, which was rejected by the popes and the Magisterium.[20]

III. The Four Causes of the Church

Before we actually discuss the four causes of the Church, we need to discuss the four causes themselves briefly. The discussion of the four causes of a thing, originated with Aristotle.[21] The first kind of cause was called the material cause and the material cause is "that out of which a thing is made."[22] For example, bronze is the material out of which a statue is made. The next kind of cause is called a formal cause and it is "that which makes the matter be what it is."[23] Since matter is potentially an infinite number of different things and since any given matter can have a variety of different forms in it, (for example the same matter can be under the form of a dog, a cat, a human being, etc.) then the formal cause is what makes the matter be a dog, a cat or human being. In other words, what the matter becomes is determined by the formal cause. The common example given is that it is the form of the goddess Venus, when introduced into bronze, that makes it a bronze statue of Venus. The form is what makes it a statue of Venus and not something else. The third kind of cause is called the efficient cause and it is the cause which "brings the thing into existence."[24] In the case of the statue of Venus, the efficient cause is the artist who works with the bronze in order to give it the form or shape of Venus. The last kind of cause is called the final cause and it is "that for which a thing is made" or we may say "the reason the thing

---

[20] Pope Pius XII in the document *Mystici Corporis* (para. 22) continues in the same vein by observing: Quamobrem qui fide vel regimine invicem dividuntur, in uno eiusmodi Corpore, atque uno eius divino Spiritu vivere nequeunt. (It follows that those are divided in faith or government cannot be living in the unity of such a Body, nor can they be living the life of its one Divine Spirit.)

[21] These four causes are enumerated and discussed in Physics l. II, c. 3, and Metaphysics l. V, c. 2.

[22] Wuellner, *A Dictionary of Scholastic Philosophy*, p. 181 and Coffey, *Ontology*, p. 364

[23] See Wuellner, *A Dictionary of Scholastic Philosophy*, p. 106 under "form."

[24] See Wuellner, *A Dictionary of Scholastic Philosophy*, p. 42 under "cause."

is made."[25]

Garrigou-Lagrange in his work *De Revelatione*[26] observes how the four marks of the Church correlate to the four causes as enumerated by Aristotle. He observes that the "*catholic unity* denotes the form and matter of the Church."[27] Here two causes come together just as in the example of matter and form above, as the bronze and the form of Venus come together to constitute the statue of Venus. So in the case of the Church, the matter, "that out of which the Church is made," is its Catholicity, i.e. the various members from different races and nations throughout the world. The formal cause is the unity of the Church. This is based upon the fact that the form is that which unifies the matter into one being. So, it is the oneness of the Church (under one head,[28] i.e. government, one faith, etc.) which constitutes the formal cause. The efficient cause is the apostolicity of the Church. The apostolicity of the Church is constituted by the apostolic succession, both material and formal,[29] when those who participate in apostolic succession use of the elements of sanctification, such as baptism, etc., causing the existence of the Church.[30] The final cause of the Church is its holiness; it is the reason

---

[25] See Wuellner, *A Dictionary of Scholastic Philosophy*, p. 90 under "end."

[26] Vol. II, p. 256. Journet, *Church of the Word Incarnate*, p. XXVI refers to Garrigou Lagrange as linking up the properties and notes with the four causes of the Church: "In this perspective the four marks, the four notes of the church, naturally fall into place as corollaries of each of our four causes respectively. They are seen as rooted in and growing out of the very essence of the Church, and exteriorization, a normal manifestation, of her ministry." The term "notes" is also used to refer to the marks of the Church.

[27] Garrigou Lagrange, *De Revelatione*, loc. cit.: Catholica unitas denotat formam et materiam Ecclesiae.

[28] Leo XIII, *Satis Cognitum*, para. 13: mide unitas exorta, quia in christiana republica causa efficiens unitatis est Ecclesia romana (the source of unity, because the Roman Church is the efficient cause of unity in the Christian commonwealth).

[29] See OCE, vol. 1, p. 648 under "apostolicity."

[30] Obviously the apostolicity is a secondary efficient cause of the Church's existence. The primary efficient cause would be God Himself. Unlike the Protestants who would only hold to the primary cause, the Catholic Church would recognize that there is a secondary efficient cause of the Church's

why God brings the Church into existence, sanctifying its members and has a holy doctrine and the elements of sanctification.

As the theologians and the Church herself have pointed out, the Roman Catholic Church is the only one that has all four marks.[31] In addition to having all four marks, each of the marks or notes are only had in their true and proper sense within the Roman Catholic Church.[32] So that even when other religions have various aspects of the marks or notes, they do not have them in their true, proper or full sense.

IV. Principle of the Integral Good in Relation to the Mark of Unity

A. God as an Integral Cause

When the cause of the Church is considered, it can only be God and this follows from several principles. The first is the nature of God's causation.

> Evil which consists in a defect of action, is always caused by a defect of the agent. In God, however, there is no defect but the highest perfection... Hence evil which consists in a defect of action, or which is caused from a defect of the agent, is not reduced to God as in a cause.[33]

When considering God as cause, everything He causes is good and if there is any defect in a thing, it is the result of a created agent which lacks some perfection or we may say it is not in the primary cause but in the existence.

---

[31]Among other, see Berry, *The Church of Christ*, p. 148.

[32]Deickmann, *De Ecclesia*, p. 497: notae verae Ecclesiae Christi verificantur in sola Ecclesia romano-catholica.

[33]ST I, q. 49, a. 2: Malum quod in defectu actionis consistit, semper causatur ex defectu agentis. In Deo autem nullus defectus est, sed summa perfectio, ut supra ostensum est. Unde malum quod in defectu actionis consistit, vel quod ex defectu agentis causatur, non reducitur in Deum sicut in causam. Further in this question he observes that God is the cause of evil but not intending it *per se* but *per accidens* insofar as He wishes the punishment of those who do evil, etc. This is why it is said God does not will or cause evil, but permits it.

secondary cause to which the defect or evil is reduced.

This is based on several principles:

> 1) the principle of operation (*agere sequitur esse*): being follows upon action; how a being acts is determined by its nature: God is perfect, therefore everything He does is perfect both in its action and in its effect;
>
> 2) the principle of resemblance (variant): a cause is always some way in the effect; God who is perfect when causing a thing, He always causes it to be perfect or good;[34]
>
> 3) evils arise from the deficient operation of finite causes.[35]

It is based on these principles that one must see a first principle which is derived from the other first principles, viz. God acts integrally, or we may say: God is an integral cause. What this essentially means is that any time God constitutes a thing in the beginning in which there are no other secondary causes involved, that thing is perfect in its nature. Another way of saying it is that God never causes a deficient or defect thing when He is the only cause and the only time a thing is defective or deficient is when there is a secondary cause, i.e. when a secondary cause introduces that defect or potency into the effect.

B. The Catholic Church as Caused by God

The foundation of the Church, in effect its creation, is caused by God and from this one must logically draw the conclusion that only that

---

[34] This does not mean that things that exist that have evil in them are not caused by God; God still causes the existence of the thing which is a good or perfection; the defect is introduced on the side of the secondary cause.

[35] SSP, p. 199, n. 200.

Church, of which God is the sole cause, can be said to be perfect.[36] In order for a Church to be perfect, it must come directly from God at its institution since only He is an integral cause in the process of creating a church. Any other religion which does not come directly from God (i.e. Christ[37]), will have secondary causes or agents, i.e. humans, as its cause. Since they are not perfect, they are incapable of begetting a church that is perfect. Since no other church can claim to have God as its sole cause but was started by human beings who were not God, such as Martin Luther, Henry VIII, Mohammed, etc., no other church is integrally caused. This is why the theologians point out that: "The *integral* note is a note which is taken according to their visible characters. We concede some effigy of the notes in other churches, but [they are] truly lacking, or more or less well truncated."[38] None of the other churches can be said to have even one of the notes in its fullest sense but it indicates that none of the other Churches are part of the divinely established means of salvation.

This is based upon the following observation and principle: "the Catholic Church manifests all full four notes. No other Church manifests the full four notes. No full note is found in any other Christian group which is outside of the Catholic Church."[39] This observation that only the Catholic Church has any one of the notes fully and that it alone has all

---

[36] By saying that the Church is perfect, we have in mind here both Pius XI's (loc. cit.) and Pius XII's discussion of it as a perfect society. It was entirely disingenuous for theologians after the document *Mystici Corporis Christi* to mock Pius XII (and Pius XI for that matter) by asserting that the humans which are part of the Church are not perfect. They knew full well that by perfect society he was not referring to the perfections of the members but to the perfection of the Church as having all necessary elements to be a full and complete society in the proper sense, i.e. lacking nothing that is necessary to being a complete society.

[37] That Christ started the Church see Leo XIII, *Satis Cognitum*, passim.

[38] Lutz, Tractatus de Ecclesia Christi, p. 170: *Integra nota est nota secundum suos characteres visibiles sumpta. Concedimus autem esse in alias Ecclesiis aliquam effigiem notarum, sed valde mancam, seu plus minusve bene truncatam.* - emphasis his.

[39] Lutz, Tractatus de Ecclesia Christi, p. 170f: Pars I. Ecclesia Catholica cunctis quatuor notis conspicua est. Pars II. Nulla alia Ecclesia cunctis quartuor notis conspicua est. Pars III. Nulla nota integra invenitur in ulla coetu christiano, qui est extra ecclesiam Catholicam.

four notes indicates that only it has God as its cause. Since God is an integral cause and since the Church which God causes must be perfect in its institution, then only that Church which has all four causes (four notes) which come together in the one Church can claim to be the Church which God established.

When we consider this in light of the principle of the excluded middle, we begin to see something else that is important. The principle of the excluded middle states: A thing must either be or not be at the same time and in the same respect or relation.[40] This is sometimes formulated as: either a thing is or it is not. The variant of this principles states: there is no intermediate or mean between being and non-being nor between any pair of contradictories.[41] When applying this principle to the Church, we see that either a church is part of the Catholic Church, i.e. the Church that God established, or it is not. There cannot be varying degrees of participation based upon the principle of God as an integral cause, the doctrine that God established the Church directly and the principle of excluded middle. For this reason, we see that the Branch Theory is entirely untenable and assuming the doctrine that God established the Church directly, it is irrational[42] to assert that other religions or churches which are not in union with the Catholic Church are part of the Church which Christ established.

The union with the Church is seen in the context of what was delineated above, viz. that one must be in union with *the* principle of unity, i.e. the office of the papacy and not lack any of the other principles of unity (each constitute *a* principle of unity), viz. government, faith or sacraments. Schism by its very nature is against unity with the Church, specifically submission to the Petrine office, so it cannot be said that the schismatic churches which have material apostolic succession are in union with the Church which Christ established. In fact, the Orthodox by holding that it is through apostolicity that one "participates" in the Church of Christ essentially collapsed the mark of unity into the mark of apostolicity. Essentially they said that one is joined to the Church which Christ established by apostolic succession. While it is true apostolic

---

[40] Wuellner, op. cit., p. 35, n. 34.

[41] Ibid.

[42] To deny a first principles or to think contrary to a first principle was always considered in the Aristotelian/scholastic tradition to be irrational.

succession is part of the government by bishops and it is even part of the sacraments, these are not *the* principle of unity. Moreover, the Branch Theory or the theory of participation in the Church of Christ as long as one's church has material apostolic succession is directly contrary to the principle of excluded middle. Since their governments are not under the Petrine office and since their faith is not integral,[43] there are contradictions between the Roman Catholic Church and these religions. For that reason, the principle of excluded middle denies any *participation* in the Church which Christ established of those external to it or outside of it. This is also why the Mystical Body of Christ is identical with the Catholic Church because none of the other religions are part of it due to the principle of excluded middle and due to the fact that they are not part of the religion which has God as its cause, but are parts of religions which have taken certain elements from the Catholic Church but introduced (through humans as secondary causes) other elements (i.e. defects).

By default then, it must also be concluded that one must hold to the entirety of what the Catholic Church proposes as necessary for assent in order to be part of the Church God caused. Any deviation violates the requirement of integrity of faith as *a* principle of unity. St. Thomas observes based upon the convertibility of the transcendentals that, "the true and the good in the [same] subject are convertible."[44] Since the true and the good are one, we can say that truth also adheres to the principle of the integral good, i.e. a proposition or thing is not true if it lacks one of the causes necessary for it to be integral. We know this by the natural inclination (natural law) when we recognize that something is not true, e.g. if one were to say that the grass outside is green and lush. If the grass is not lush, while the rest of the proposition may contain the truth insofar as the grass is green, taken as a whole, the statement is false. In relation to a church not in union with the Catholic Church, one may say,

---

[43] Both the Anglicans and the Orthodox hold teachings contrary to the teaching of the Roman Catholic Church. As St. Thomas observes in the *Catena Aurea in Lucam* (l. 17, c. 5): quisquis ergo in ecclesiae societate doctrinam integram veramque assequitur, eo quod manifestetur. Pius XII (*Satis Cognitum*, para. 8) teaches: "It was thus the duty of all who heard Jesus Christ, if they wished for eternal salvation, not merely to accept His doctrine as a whole, but to assent with their entire mind to all and every point of it, since it is unlawful to withhold faith from God even in regard to one single point."

[44] ST II-II, 109, 2, ad 1: Verum et bonum subiecto quidem convertuntur.

therefore, based upon convertibility, that these religions are not true because they do not adhere either in doctrine and morals with the Catholic Church or they lack some cause (note or aspect of a note) in the Church that God established. This is why the Catholic Church is the only divinely established means of salvation,[45] because all other religions, due

---

[45]Under "Church" from the OCE we read: VI. THE NECESSARY MEANS OF SALVATION: In the preceding examination of the Scriptural doctrine regarding the Church, it has been seen how clearly it is laid down that only by entering the Church can we participate in the redemption wrought for us by Christ. Incorporation with the Church can alone unite us to the family of the second Adam, and alone can engraft us into the true Vine. Moreover, it is to the Church that Christ has committed those means of grace through which the gifts He earned for men are communicated to them. The Church alone dispenses the sacraments. It alone makes known the light of revealed truth. Outside the Church these gifts cannot be obtained. From all this there is but one conclusion: Union with the Church is not merely one out of various means by which salvation may be obtained: it is the only means.

This doctrine of the absolute necessity of union with the Church was taught in explicit terms by Christ. Baptism, the act of incorporation among her members, He affirmed to be essential to salvation. "He that believeth and is baptized shall be saved: he that believeth not shall be condemned" (Mark, xvi, 16). Any disciple who shall throw off obedience to the Church is to be reckoned as one of the heathen: he has no part in the kingdom of God (Matt., xviii, 17). St. Paul is equally explicit. "A man that is a heretic," he writes to Titus, "after the first and second admonition avoid, knowing that he that is such a one is . . . condemned by his own judgment" (Tit., iii, 10 sq.). The doctrine is summed up in the phrase, Extra Ecclesiam nulla salus...

It is instructive to observe that this doctrine has been proclaimed at every period of the Church's history. It is no accretion of a later age. The earliest successors of the Apostles speak as plainly as the medieval theologians, and the medieval theologians are not more emphatic than those of today. From the first century to the twentieth there is absolute unanimity. St. Ignatius of Antioch writes: "Be not deceived, my brethren. If any man followeth one that maketh schism, he doth not inherit the kingdom of God. If any one walketh in strange doctrine, he hath no fellowship with the Passion" (ad Philad., n. 3). Origen says: "Let no man deceive himself. Outside this house, i.e. outside the Church, none is saved" (Hom. in Jos., iii, n. 5 in P. G., XII, 841). St. Cyprian speaks to the same effect: "He cannot have God for his father, who has not the Church for his mother" (De Unit., c. vi). The words of the Fourth Ecumenical Council of Lateran (1215) define the doctrine thus in its decree against the Albigenses: "Una est fidelium universalis Ecclesia, extra quam nullus omnino salvatur" (Denzinger, n. 357); and Pius IX employed almost identical language in his Encyclical to the

to having man as their cause, lack an integral cause.[46]

V. Further Conclusions

If we return to the consideration from a prior chapter about *communicatio in sacris*, we begin to see why many after Vatican II began holding that one can have *communicatio in sacris* with non-Catholics. As was noted in the prior chapter, to join your prayers with someone who is visibly outside the Church is to join your prayers to someone, at least on an external level, who is outside the Church which Christ established. Since we cannot determine the person's will, in order not to offend God, we cannot join our prayers to his, assuming that visible separation also means a non-acceptance of the government, faith and/or sacraments of the Church.

However, after Vatican II, *communicatio in sacris* was believed to be possible in many people's minds because they adopted the Branch Theory, the teaching of the Orthodox about unity through apostolicity or a combination or a variation of the two. They thought these other churches were part of the Church since they "participated" in the one Church of Christ, because they had some semblance of one or more of the notes, they then concluded that they were part of the Church and so you could pray with them. However, as was shown above, inclusion in the Church is subject to the principle of excluded middle: either the Orthodox and the Anglicans are part of the Church which Christ established or they are not. If the Catholic Church is the Church which God established and if these other religions possess teachings contrary to what the Catholic Church either teaches or holds, i.e. if they do not accept the teaching of the Catholic Church whole and entire, by virtue of that very contradiction, they are excluded from the Church which Christ

---

bishops of Italy (10 August, 1863): "Notissimum est catholicum dogma neminem scilicet extra catholicam ecclesiam posse salvari" (Denzinger, n. 1529).

[46] The question of whether a particular religion is part of the Church which Christ established is a separate question from the status of the members of other religions in relation to their possibility of salvation or even membership in the Catholic Church.

established.[47]

---

[47] Once the Branch Theory was adopted and it began to be taught that one could have *communicatio in sacris* with the Orthodox or those who had valid material apostolic succession, the reasons behind why it was considered permissible were not transmitted well and so it resulted in a variety of practices in regard to *communicatio in sacris* with various denominations other than the Orthodox and the Anglicans.

Chapter 5: Evolution

I. Initial Observations

The relationship between the evolutionary hypothesis and the historicity of the first three chapters of Genesis has a long and involved history, but the Pontifical Biblical Commission has already made a ruling.[1] There was a widespread rejection of the literal sense of the first three books of Genesis by the denial of the proposition that the first three books of Genesis contained actual historical events. The rejection of the historicity of the first three books of Genesis is motivated by a basic worldliness and by that is meant a desire to conform the Scriptures and theology to the hypotheses present within the world and by the scientific community of the day.

It is for this reason that we read in the documents of Vatican I:

> We also reject and condemn by an anathema the doctrine which asserts the treatment of the natural and rational sciences so that it were necessary to be of their own right and plainly independent, that propositions (*sententiae*) which in them are established and deduced, although contrary to the Catholic doctrine, are not under the judgment and authentic proscription of the Church and therefore the natural and rational sciences also with their

---

[1] "Concerning the Historical Character of the First Three Chapters of Genesis", A.A.S. 1 [1909] 567ff (June 30, 1909). Also found in Denz. 2121ff.

> differences are to be treated as errors contrary to the Catholic faith and doctrine, which bear no resemblance to supernatural revelation.[2]

Essentially what the Church has defined is that it is entirely within its right to pass judgment on the propositions of the natural sciences, if these propositions are contrary to Catholic doctrine. This means that it is within the right of the Church to pass judgment on those aspects of the evolutionary hypothesis which are contrary to Catholic doctrine. The First Vatican Council goes on to say:

> If anyone says that it is possible that at some time, given the advancement of science (*scientiae*), a sense may be assigned to the dogmas propounded by the Church which is different from that which the Church has understood and understands: let him be anathema.[3]

Essentially what the Church is saying between these two citations is that if a natural or rational science concludes something that is contrary to the faith, the natural or rational science is to be considered in error. Furthermore, the Church is not to be expected to conform its teachings regarding doctrine to the hypotheses of the natural or rational sciences.[4]

---

[2] Vatican I, *Filius Dei*, chpt. 4, para. 9: Reprobamus itaque et anathemate damnamus doctrinam qua asseritur tractationem scientiarum naturalium et rationalium ita sui iuris et plane independentem esse oportere ut sententiae quae in illis statuuntur et deducuntur etiamsi doctrinae catholicae repugnent non subsint iudicio et authenticae proscriptioni ecclesiae atque ideo scientias naturales et rationales etiam sub discrimine in eis errandi contra fidem et doctrinam Catholicam tractandas esse nulla supernaturalis revelationis habita ratione.

[3] Ibid., can. 3: Si quis dixerit fieri posse ut dogmatibus ab ecclesia propositis aliquando secundum progressum scientiae sensus tribuendus sit alius ab eo quem intellexit et intelligit ecclesia, anathema sit.

[4] If one holds to the opposite, viz. that Catholic doctrine must conform to the natural and rational sciences, in the end, the evolutionary hypothesis will destroy the credibility of Scripture; it will attempt to reinterpret Genesis as allegory, myth, etc.; it will deviate, subvert and reject the authority of the Fathers of the Church since it will reject how they have always understood the act of creation, resulting in a rejection of the vast majority of Catholic doctrine,

Part of the reason has to do with where the greater certainty lies. Ever since Descartes, greater certitude has been ascribed to mathematics or certain rational or natural sciences than to theology or even to metaphysics (philosophy). However, St. Thomas observes something very important regarding certitude:

> Nothing prohibits that which is more certain according to nature, to be with respect to us, less certain because of the weakness of our intellect which "relates to those things most manifest in nature, as the eye of the owl to the light of the sun"... Hence the doubt which happens in some people about articles of faith, is not because of the incertitude of the thing, but because of the weakness of the human intellect.[5]

Regarding matters of the faith, many of them are actually more certain than those things which pertain to the natural or rational sciences. In another place,[6] St. Thomas observes that faith is actually more certain on the side of the cause, viz. God than what pertains to those things which we know through our own human endeavors.

On the side of those who want to be able to conform Catholic doctrine and the Scriptures to the evolutionary hypothesis through what has now become known as "continuous creation,"[7] they admit: "the concept of continuous creation does not appear in the texts of the

---

Scripture and Tradition. Part of the reason for the Church's reluctance to pass judgment has to do with the Galileo affair. However, regardless of the historical facts in that particular case, it does not detract from the Church's right to pass judgment on those matters which pertain to or touch upon Revelation.

[5]ST I, q. 1, a. 5, ad 2: nihil prohibet id quod est certius secundum naturam, esse quoad nos minus certum, propter debilitatem intellectus nostri, qui se habet ad manifestissima naturae, sicut oculus noctuae ad lumen solis... Unde dubitatio quae accidit in aliquibus circa articulos fidei, non est propter incertitudinem rei, sed propter debilitatem intellectus humani.

[6]ST II-II, q. 4, a. 8.

[7]Continuous creation is the notion that creation did not cease with the first six days but continues even now as God continues to create new creatures through the process of evolution.

Magisterium of the Catholic Church, it is not present among the mediaevals, nor among the Fathers of the Church, but one is able to find express precursors."[8] Effectively speaking, Revol admits that the idea of continuous creation which is necessary for a theistic evolutionary hypothesis in which God must continually create new creatures, even after the initial creation in the beginning, is not to be found anywhere in the Magisterium of the Church, among medieval theological schools or the Fathers of the Church. On a certain level, this should be the end of the discussion. However, the motivation behind wanting to conform the interpretation of the first three books of Genesis to the evolutionary hypothesis is driven by this desire to conform Catholic doctrine, Scriptures, etc. as much as possible to the natural and rational sciences.

It should be observed that elsewhere the idea of theistic evolution was already addressed in relationship to it being a violation of the principle of economy.[9] However, it should be noted that the notion of continuous creation, which will be dealt with more below, essentially asserts that there are constant miracles. However, the very nature of a miracle is that it is the exception and not the rule, because it is a suspension of the law of nature, which is the rule. Creation by its definition of bringing something out of nothing on the part of God is a miracle and therefore is not the rule. It is for this reason that St. Thomas says: "God acts in every way, by conserving and administering the established creature, not however in creating a new creature."[10] We shall address this further below but we can also observe that this is why Scripture says that God *rested*[11] after He had created, indicating that there was a cessation of creation and after that His creation entered into the

---

[8] Revol, *Le Temps de la Création*, p. 18: Le concept de création continuée n'apparaît pas dans les textes du magistère de l'Église catholique, il n'est pas présent non plus chez les médiévaux, ni chez les Pères de l'Église bien qu'il soit possible d'en trouver des énoncés précurseurs.

[9] See Ripperger, *Metaphysics of Evolution*, p. 53-59.

[10] ST I , q. 73, q. 2, ad 1: Deus usque modo operatur, conservando et administrando creaturam conditam, non autem novam creaturam condendo.

[11] Genesis 2:1f: Igitur perfecti sunt caeli et terra et omnis ornatus eorum complevitque. Deus die septimo opus suum quod fecerat et *requievit* die septimo ab universo opere quod patrarat.

time of providence and conservation.[12] Specifically, this meant that the activity of creation on the part of God did not continue.

When one considers the rational sciences, viz. philosophy, specifically after the time of Descartes but including Hegel, Hume, etc. one is struck by a few facts. The first is the fact that many who were proponents of the evolutionary hypothesis were deists,[13] e.g. James Hutton, Jean Baptiste de Lamarck, Charles Darwin[14] and Charles Lyell, among others. Deism is a philosophical system which generally holds that God created the universe and set it in motion but then had no interaction with what He had created. One can see how the evolutionary hypothesis arose out of this philosophical framework since there has to be some accounting for how the various things came to be if one is going to exclude God, as a general rule, from that process.

Second, one is also struck by the fact that many of those who were proponents of evolution were also freemasons or influenced by freemasonry, such as Charles Darwin,[15] Erasmus Darwin and James Hutton as well as possibly Alfred Russell Wallace.[16] When one examines the freemasonic doctrines, it becomes clear that it is essentially a form of

---

[12] Throughout the doctrinal history of the Church, after creation was completed, it was held that God then conserved His creation in being and then administered it or took care of it as to His providential plan. For example, see De Pot., q. 5, a. 1, ad 2.

[13] For a good synopsis of Deism, see OCE under Deism. For a list of deists, see https://en.wikipedia.org/wiki/List_of_deists

[14] Darwin's position is essentially Deist, believing in the first cause while at the same time believing that the evolutionary process was driven by natural selection.

[15] Mackey's Encyclopedia of Freemasonry, "The name of Charles Darwin does not appear on the rolls of the Lodge but it is very possible that he, like Francis, was a Mason." Even if he was not a Freemason, he would have been influenced by freemasonry being raised by his father who was a Freemason as well as at least the writings of his grandfather, who he never knew and who was also Freemason.

[16] This may be found by any cursory search on the internet.

Gnosticism.[17] In fact, by asserting that death is an integral part of the evolutionary process in the coming into being of the various natures of things, one sees that evolution is simply a subtle form of Manichaeism[18] in which evil is simply part of creation. Unlike the Catholic doctrine in which creation resulted in God creating something that was good, of which evil was not a part, evolution needs evil, death and destruction as part of the process. We see that in varying forms of the evolutionary hypothesis, such as Darwinism which holds that there is a selection of the fittest, which results in those who are unfit dying or being removed from the process of passing on genetic code to offspring.

II. Some Thomistic Citations in Relationship to Creation

There is a quotation from St. Thomas which is worthy of noting despite its length:

> That the world not always was, is held only by faith and is not able to be demonstrated as also above it was said of the mystery of the Trinity. And the reason is that the newness of the world is not able to be demonstrated on the part of the world itself. For the principle of demonstration is that which is.[19] However, each thing, according to the notion of its species, is abstracted from the here and now, because of which it is said that the universals are everywhere and always. Hence it is not able to be demonstrated that man, or the heavens, or a stone not always was. Similarly also neither on the part of the agent, which acts through the will. For the will of God is not able to be investigated by reason, except about

---

[17]That the freemasons themselves see their origins from the gnostics, see OCE under Freemasonry.

[18]See OCE under Manichaeism: As the theory of two eternal principles, good and evil, is predominant in this fusion of ideas and gives color to the whole, Manichaeism is classified as a form of religious Dualism.

[19]The Latin for the phrase "that which is" is *quod quid est*, which is the literalization of the term used by Aristotle to indicate the essence of the thing.

that which it is absolutely necessary for God to will, however, this does not apply to creatures, as was said. However, the divine will is able to be manifested to man by revelation, on which faith depends. Hence it is credible that the world began to be, however it is not demonstratable or knowable. And this is useful to be considered, lest perhaps someone, presuming to demonstrate it is of the faith, does not induce necessary reasons, which offer material to the laughter of infidels, judging us because of these reasons to believe that they are of the faith.[20]

St. Thomas says that the world began to be and was created anew is not something that we should presume can be demonstrated by the natural light of reason, lest we end up succumbing to the derision of those who do not believe.[21] In other words, one must be aware of whether an audience is going to accept a particular argument or not.

When considering the discussion at hand, this essentially means that we can only have certitude regarding many matters pertaining to creation by the light of faith and from the Church's *de fide* definitions that the world was created *ex nihilo* by God, etc. This does not mean that we do not hold that the world depends upon God as its cause for its

---

[20]ST I, q. 46, a. 2: quod mundum non semper fuisse, sola fide tenetur, et demonstrative probari non potest, sicut et supra de mysterio Trinitatis dictum est. Et huius ratio est, quia novitas mundi non potest demonstrationem recipere ex parte ipsius mundi. Demonstrationis enim principium est quod quid est. Unumquodque autem, secundum rationem suae speciei, abstrahit ab hic et nunc, propter quod dicitur quod universalia sunt ubique et semper. Unde demonstrari non potest quod homo, aut caelum, aut lapis non semper fuit. Similiter etiam neque ex parte causae agentis, quae agit per voluntatem. Voluntas enim Dei ratione investigari non potest, nisi circa ea quae absolute necesse est Deum velle, talia autem non sunt quae circa creaturas vult, ut dictum est. Potest autem voluntas divina homini manifestari per revelationem, cui fides innititur. Unde mundum incoepisse est credibile, non autem demonstrabile vel scibile. Et hoc utile est ut consideretur, ne forte aliquis, quod fidei est demonstrare praesumens, rationes non necessarias inducat, quae praebeant materiam irridendi infidelibus, existimantibus nos propter huiusmodi rationes credere quae fidei sunt.

[21]We shall prescind from the lengthy discussion about whether an infinite regress as possible.

existence, as this can be known by the natural light of reason. This also does not mean that we cannot give reasonable demonstrations or even arguments which support the fact that the world was created in a short period of time, but we would not say that they are demonstrated with certainty, except by the Church's teaching. Moreover, this also does not mean that we cannot use arguments and demonstrations to show that the evolutionary hypothesis is untenable through the natural light of reason or by scientific investigation, since many of its assertions cannot be demonstrated either scientifically or philosophically or can even be proven to be false. In fact, many times they are contrary to reason, which has been seen in relationship to the violation of the first principles.[22]

What is important to note here is that *how* things began, i.e. how things were created can only be known through Revelation because the creation itself, the natural world itself, does not contain within it sufficient information to deduce how it came to be. Nature does, however, contain sufficient information to exclude various aspects of the evolutionary hypothesis, on a scientific basis as well as on a philosophical basis.[23] It is for this reason that one is bound by the teaching of the Church regarding those doctrines of creation, i.e. that the world was created *ex nihilo*,[24] that it was created together and in a short period of time,[25] that there was no pre-existing matter, that the doctrine of Original Sin is to be held, etc. because we cannot have certainty about how things were created purely by the natural light of reason. It is for this reason that any conclusions contrary to the teaching of the Church regarding creation must be held to be in error, since ultimately the only way the truth can be known is through Revelation and the judgment regarding matters of Revelation pertaining to the Magisterium of the Roman

---

[22] Cf. Ripperger, *Metaphysics of Evolution*, passim.

[23] The truth of this proposition is exhibited by the fact that, even within the context of the evolutionary hypothesis, there have been numerous changes regarding time lines, interpretation of stratification, contravening evidence in the fossil record, etc. If this was merely a matter of actual science and could be known with certainty, then the constant shifting around and modification of the hypothesis itself would not be required.

[24] Vatican I, *Filius Dei* (Denz. 1805). See also Ott, *Fundamentals of Catholic Dogma*, p. 79.

[25] Owen, "The Traditional Catholic Doctrine of Creation."

Catholic Church.

Now, we turn our attention to certain things that we can know about creation as well as to demonstrat certain things that are contrary to reason and sound theology regarding creation.[26] Let us begin by noting a section from St. Thomas from his disputed questions on truth:

> Every nature is created by God immediately according to its first institution.[27] Moreover one creature is able to be moved by another, presupposing the natural powers of each creature attributed to divine work. And therefore we posit that the celestial bodies are the causes of the inferior [bodies] by way of motion alone. And thus to be a medium in the work of governance, not however the works of creation.[28]

This observation along with the fact that God, in creating, does so without motion[29] indicates that there are no secondary causes involved in the process of creation. The evolutionary hypothesis in relationship to macro evolution by its very nature asserts that there are secondary causes in the coming into being of new species (nature). Motion, the reduction of something from potency to act,[30] involves a process and creation is specifically something which does not involve a process but is merely God bringing the thing from nothing directly into existence. Creation can therefore refer to two things: (1) the creation of a specific nature and in this case it does not involve a process; (2) the totality of all of the things

---

[26]The extensive discussion that has already been had regarding scientific problems of evolution will not be addressed here.

[27]The word *institution* in this context means establishment or creation.

[28]De Ver., q. 5, a. 9: omnem naturam immediate esse a Deo conditam secundum sui primam institutionem. Unam autem creaturam moveri ab altera, praesuppositis virtutibus naturalibus utrique creaturae ex divino opere attributis; et ideo ponimus corpora caelestia esse causas inferiorum per viam motus tantum; et sic esse media in opere gubernationis,
non autem in opere creationis.

[29]SCG II, c. 17.

[30]Wuellner, *A Dictionary of Scholastic Philosophy*, p. 195

that are brought into existence, e.g. when we use the term *creation* to refer to the totality of everything that exists other than God. In the second case, we can say that there is a process but not in the sense of motion in the creation of species insofar as God begins by creating first the earth and the heavens, then plants, then animals, then man.[31] Only in relationship to man does the book of Genesis give an indication that God used pre-existing matter to create the body of Adam.[32] The point being is that in the initial creation of specific natures, there is not anything pre-existing and therefore there is no involvement of secondary causes in the bringing of these things into existence. The only exception is Adam's body but even that comes from the earth, which did not pre-exist as God created it from nothing.[33]

St. Thomas observes that "it is not necessary that the diversity of things is from matter but from divine wisdom, which instituted the complete universe of diverse natures."[34] In the mind of St. Thomas, the matter, or we may even say the material causes, cannot be the reason for why there is such diversity in things. Rather, it comes from the divine wisdom[35] and this can be known by the complexity of the order of the universe and how there is a gradation of being from the bottom to the top without any gaps[36] as well as how this diversity of being works together and the different creatures are ordered towards each other.

In the *Summa Theologiae*, we read:
to create pertains only to God. Hence those which are

---

[31] This is the progression that is seen in the book of Genesis.

[32] It should be noted that Genesis specifically says that God went back to the earth and not to an animal to provide the matter for Adam's body.

[33] For further citations that there were not secondary causes involved in the process of creation in St. Thomas' works, see De Pot, q. 3, a.1, especially ad 2 and ST I, q. 45, a. 5.

[34] De Pot., q. 3, a. 1, ad 9: et ideo diversitas rerum non oportet quod sit ex materia, sed ex ordine divinae sapientiae; quae ad complementum universi diversas naturas instituit.

[35] See also ST I, q. 47, a. 2.

[36] This is known as the principle of hierarchy of being, see SSP, p. 209, n. 210.

not able to be caused except by creation, are produced only by God, and these are those things which are not subject to generation and corruption. Secondly, since according to this position, the universe of things does not arise from the intention of the first agent, but from a combination of agents of multiple causes. We say that such a thing arises from chance. Thus therefore the completion of the universe, which consists in the diversity of things, is from chance, which is impossible. Hence it is to be said that the distinction and multitude of things is from the intention of the primary agent, which is God.[37]

In the mind of St. Thomas, because creation is not part of the process of generation[38] and corruption,[39] creation is not subject to the evolutionary process. To formulate it another way, the coming about of new species (nature) is not subject to the evolutionary process but only to the creative power alone by which God brings the thing immediately into existence from nothing.

III. The Principle of the Integral Good in Creation

Scripture recounts, "and God saw all the things that He had made, and they were very good."[40] The fact that what God had made was good means that the principle of the integral good also applies to creation. We

---

[37] ST I, q. 47, a. 1: Creare solius Dei est. Unde ea quae non possunt causari nisi per creationem, a solo Deo producuntur, et haec sunt omnia quae non subiacent generationi et corruptioni. Secundo, quia secundum hanc positionem, non proveniret ex intentione primi agentis universitas rerum, sed ex concursu multarum causarum agentium. Tale autem dicimus provenire a casu. Sic igitur complementum universi, quod in diversitate rerum consistit, esset a casu, quod est impossibile. Unde dicendum est quod distinctio rerum et multitudo est ex intentione primi agentis, quod est Deus.

[38] Generation is the natural process by which something comes into existence presupposing secondary causes.

[39] The process by which something goes out of existence.

[40] Genesis 1: 31.

read in the *Summa* the following:

> Since the completion which is according to the integrity of the parts of the universe suits the sixth day, the consummation which is according to operation of the parts suits the seventh. Or it is able to be said that in continuous motion sometimes something is able to be moved further, it is not called perfect motion before the quiet, for the quiet demonstrates the completion of motion. Moreover, God was able to make more creatures, other than those which He made in the six days. Hence, it is said that his work was completed when he ceased to create new creatures on the seventh day.[41]

Essentially what St. Thomas is saying is that the work of creation ceased at the end of the sixth day. Scripture essentially reveals that creation ended on the sixth day[42] and that on the seventh day God rested and it is at that time that providence and conservation of being begin. This means that the diversity of creatures which we find in the created order is due to God's creative activity which ceased after the sixth day which does not envision an evolutionary process, not just because as we saw above there are no secondary causes in the act of creation, because the actual creation of a new species or new kinds of creatures terminated at that time. Given what is revealed, theistic evolution cannot be tenable insofar as creation is an act of God and terminates at a certain point and thus theistic evolution is subject to the criticism of violating the first principles of

---

[41]ST I, q. 69, a. 2: ad 2:quia consummatio quae est secundum integritatem partium universi, competit sextae diei, consummatio quae est secundum operationem partium, competit septimae. Vel potest dici quod in motu continuo, quandiu aliquid potest moveri ulterius, non dicitur motus perfectus ante quietem, quies enim demonstrat motum consummatum. Deus autem poterat plures creaturas facere, praeter illas quas fecerat sex diebus. Unde hoc ipso quod cessavit novas creaturas condere in septima die, dicitur opus suum consummasse.

[42]What constitutes a day, whether 24 hours or a short period of time, is in the history of theology legitimately open to discussion. The Pontifical Biblical Commission admitted as much (see citation above). However, it would not be an extended period of time, as discussed at the Fourth Lateran Council and it would not include ongoing macro evolution.

metaphysics.[43] Also given what is revealed, a theistic evolution is untenable insofar as the constant miracles or the continuous creation is explicitly denied by the termination or cessation of God's creative activity.

St. Thomas observes that the "first perfection, which is the integrity of the universe, was in the first institution of things. And this is assigned to the seventh day."[44] For St. Thomas, the cessation of creative activity on the side of God and the fact that creation was good means that the creation of God was integrally good. That integral good is understood in two ways:

> For speaking according to Augustine, the twofold perfection of a thing is to be distinguished. For one is the perfection of the totality which the thing has from this that from all of its essential parts it is integrated; and such is the perfection of the world which suits the sixth day. Since after the first six days no creature was added to the world, which was done in no other way than in the six days, as will be clear. The other perfection of a thing which it has by reason of the end, which is the ultimate perfection. In such a perfection of the world is due to the seventh day, in which God rested from all the works in himself as in the end. But following the other saints is again to be distinguished a twofold perfection. One is the first perfection, which a thing has according to its being; and this perfection of the world is completed on the sixth day, since no part of the world is added afterwards which in the first six days proceeded in some way. The other is the second perfection which is the operation of the thing, as it is said in the second book of the *De Anima*. And such a perfection of the world was on the seventh day, since from thence the operation by which God instituted nature, began the operation of propagation in the whole universe, insofar as from the natures of things already given, other things were produced, which operation God

---

[43]See Ripperger, *Metaphysics of Evolution*, passim.

[44]ST I, q. 73, a. 1: prima autem perfectio, quae est in integritate universi, fuit in prima rerum institutione. Et haec deputatur septimo diei.

does even now in all things.[45]

When considering the perfection or good of God's creation, one is left with a twofold distinction. The first has to do with the perfection of the individual parts of creation in which in themselves they are all perfect in their institution or creation or whole. The second is how all the individual parts come together to constitute a perfect creation. The Principle of the Integral Good indicates that all of the parts must be good in order for the thing to be considered good in its totality, as we saw above. This being the case, the evolutionary hypothesis is untenable for the following reasons:

> 1. According to the evolutionary hypothesis, the initial creation of God was not integrally good as to the totality of creation because it was incomplete. In effect the gradation of being had gaps which indicated that the totality of creation was not integral.
> 2. The parts were also not integral insofar as they were evolving or we may say mutating in various degrees and steps without being complete in themselves. Putting aside the fact that the mutation is generally bad for a particular creature when it does not contribute directly to its own survival, the mutation process, whether done by punctuated equilibrium or over the course of a long time, means that God's creation is striving for its

---

[45] II Sent., d. 15, q. 3, a. 1: loquendo enim secundum Augustinum, distinguenda est rei duplex perfectio. Una enim est perfectio totalitatis, quam res habet ex hoc quod ex omnibus partibus suis essentialibus integrata est; et talis perfectio mundi, sextae diei competit: quia post sex primos dies nulla creatura mundo addita est, quae non aliquo modo in operibus sex dierum esset, ut patebit. Alia vero perfectio rei est quam habet ex ratione finis, quae est ultima perfectio: et talis perfectio mundi debetur septimae diei, in qua Deus ab omnibus operibus requievit in se sicut in fine. Sed sequendo alios sanctos, distinguenda est iterum duplex perfectio. Una est perfectio prima, quam scilicet res habet secundum esse suum; et haec perfectio mundi completa est sexta die: quia nulla pars mundi postmodum addita est quae in primis sex diebus non praecesserit aliquo modo. Alia est perfectio secunda, quae est operatio rei, ut dicitur 2 *De Anima*: et talis perfectio mundi fuit in septima die: quia ex tunc cessante operatione qua Deus naturam instituit, incepit operatio propagationis in toto universo, secundum quod ex naturis jam conditis res aliae producuntur; quam operationem in rebus omnibus Deus usque nunc facit.

completion, not in Him, but in the completion of the part. This means that creation does not possess the good integrally.

If we consider the other distinction above between the creation or institution of the various creatures in a total overall system or creation, we recognize that God first created the beings and then on the seventh day, i.e. after God's creative activity ceased, certain secondary operations or perfections of the creatures began. What is important to notice here in the mind of St. Thomas, as he is interpreting this passage of the book of Genesis, in light of what the saints and Fathers of the Church have said, is that the full activities (operations) of the creatures begin only after creation has ceased. But the evolutionary hypothesis has the activities of the creatures occurring in the creative process. What is ultimately being proposed in the evolutionary hypothesis is that the creation of God is not integrally good, because it is still trying to reach its natural perfection. When we consider the four causes of a thing and analyze God's involvement in these four causes, we are brought back to a discussion about God's causal action, as we saw in relationship to the causing of the Church.

As Aristotle enumerated, there are four causes of material thing. The first is the material cause which is that out of which a thing is made. God in the act of creation creates the matter which becomes the material cause. However, matter cannot exist without form[46] and so when God creates the matter, He also creates the form concomitantly. Since God is an infinite cause, on the side of the cause itself, i.e. on the side of God Himself, there is no extra energy or we may say act on His part that requires Him to cause a higher form as opposed to a lower form, since God's act is infinite. Therefore, it is not necessary to assert that God started out creating lower matter-form composites and then slowly developed them over the course of time by constantly introducing higher forms in a miraculous way in order to produce a more perfect creation. Such an assertion clearly violates the principle of economy, since it multiplies causes without necessity.

On the side of the efficient cause, God is the cause of the existence of a thing. Again because God is an infinite cause and is infinite act, on His part there is no greater act which is possible or required in the causing of a variety of different creatures in a short period of time (as we

---

[46]SSP, p. 172f, n. 172F.

see in material creation) or all at once (as He did with the entire hierarchy of angels). The difference of essences requiring greater existence is on the side of the effect, not on the side of the cause. In other words, God through one infinite act causes all of the variations of creatures regardless of the degree of existence necessary to actualize the essence of each of those creatures. To create a thing is to bridge the gap between nothing and something which is an infinite gap. As a result, secondary causes, which are finite,[47] cannot be the cause or create the various species because they are finite. Only God, Who is infinite, can be the sole cause of all things that are created.

As to the final cause, God created the material order to manifest His glory and perfection.[48] But according to the evolutionary hypothesis, the initial state of things, while having some manifestation of His perfection and glory, would not show His glory or His perfection integrally. In other words, God's perfection and glory are only fully manifest to the degree that creation can do so in the *completion* of the creation which did not occur, according to the evolutionary hypothesis, in the beginning.[49] To assert that God would cause something lesser than his final intention (final cause) does not bring Him greater glory; rather His glory is more manifest by the immediate creation of things in a state of reflecting His goodness to the degree that particular creation is capable of doing.

God as a cause cannot fail insofar as He is infinite in act; His creation comes about in exactly the manner in which He intends immediately when He intends it. Or, to put it another way, when He causes, the effect immediately comes into being. We saw in an earlier chapter that evil occurs from a single defect whereas the good occurs only when *many* things come together in the bringing of the thing into existence and so it takes just one single defective cause in order to

---

[47]Secondary causes, by definition, are always finite due to the their dependence on the primary cause.

[48]Ott, *Fundamentals of Catholic Dogma*, p. 81.

[49]One is struck with the impiety of such a proposition: to say that God would create a half-baked system which would only reach its perfection much later or possibly never at all since it would be in an ongoing evolutionary process is to detract from God's goodness in establishing a rightly ordered universe or creation.

introduce evil into a thing. In other words, as St. Thomas has said,[50] defects are only introduced when there is more than one cause. In the process of creation, as we have seen, there is only one cause, viz. God. Since there are no secondary causes to fail in creation, then there is no way that any defect could be part of the initial creation. This means that the evolutionary hypothesis, which specifically posits defects in creatures, either through natural selection or through the process of death, as creatures evolve towards more and more complex beings, is untenable. It is only after the Fall of Adam and Eve that evil is introduced into the created order and, as a result, defect is introduced by a secondary cause. Defects can only be introduced by secondary causes and therefore the defects in creation do not come from God and so God's initial creation contained no defects. This means that God, as an integral cause, would cause not only individual creatures which were whole and complete in themselves, but would also create a universe or total system in which the interactions of those various creatures would also be perfect. This would exclude evolution in which death is an integral part of the process. Death only enters into the world after the sin of Adam.[51] To use death indicates that God would not be an integral cause in bringing things into existence since things would be imperfect and especially if such creation were said to be gradual since the various beings would have organs and mutations which were not perfect or integral to that being.

God always acts as an integral cause (which it was seen in ecclesiology) and this applies equally to creation. From this, one is able to see that the evolutionary hypothesis is not compatible with the principle of the integral good and its application to God as the cause of the existence of things. The Church needs to reassert its right to pass judgment on the natural and rational sciences in regard to those propositions that are denying Scripture and the long-standing tradition of the interpretation of various parts of Scripture, among which are the first three books of Genesis.

---

[50] See prior chapter.

[51] Romans 5:12: sicut per unum hominem in hunc mundum peccatum intravit et per peccatum mors (as through one man sin entered into this world and through sin death).

Conclusion

While the principle of the integral good has been considered in itself as well as in several applications, it can be said that those are only a few aspects of its application. As one analyzes the various aspects of ecclesiology and evolution as well as several other aspects of society in general such as music and the media, one is struck by the shocking reality of the collapse of this principle. This applies not just to society at large but even within the Church. Yet, if the Church in its doctrine and society in the philosophical underpinnings of the social order are to recover their vigor, this principle must be recognized and embraced and the errors contrary to the principle of the integral good set aside.

Bibliography

Acta et Decreta sacrorum Conciliorum recentiorum. Collectio Lacensis. Tomus septimus. *Acta et Decreta sacrosancti oecumenici Concilii Vaticani.* Friburgi Brisgoviae. 1890.

Aertnys, I and Damen, C.. *Theologia Moralis secundum Doctrinam S. Alphonsi de Ligoria Doctoris Ecclesiae.* Editio XVII. Marietti. Italy. 1956.

Allen, Craig. "The Holy Office on Worship with Non-Catholics from 1622 to 1939" in *The Latin Mass Magazine.* Advent/Christmas 2006.

Attwater, Donald. *A Catholic Dictionary.* The MacMillan Company. NewYork. 1941.

Basic Works of Aristotle. Richard McKeon, ed. Random House. New York. 1941.

Bainvel, J. V. *De Ecclesia Christi,* Gabriel Beauchesne, ed. Paris. 1925.

Bergminham, Eric. "'Thomistic Evolution': Development of Doctrine or Diabolic Deception" as found at Kolbe Center for the Study of Creation. http://kolbecenter.org/thomistic-evolution-development-doctrine-diabolical-deception/ as of November 2017.

Berry, E. Sylvester, *The Church of Christ: An Apologetic and Dogmatic Treatise.* Mount Saint Mary's Seminary. Emmitsburg, Maryland. 1955.

Billot, Ludovico. *De Ecclesia Christi.* Tomus prior. Ed. Quinta. In Pont. Universitate Gregoriana. Roma. 1927.

Canons and Decrees of the Council of Trent. trans. By Rev. H.J. Schroeder, O.P. B. Herder Book Co., St. Louis. 1930.

Catechismus Catholicae Ecclesiae. Libreria Editrice Vaticana. 1997.

The Catholic Encyclopedia. The Gilmary Society. New York. 1929.

The Catholic Encyclopedia Dictionary. The Gilmary Society. New York. 1941.

Coffey, Peter, *Ontology, or the Theory of Being; an Introduction to General Metaphysics.* P. Smith. New York. 1938.

Cole, Basil. *Music and Morals: A Theological Appraisal of the Moral and Psychological Effects of Music.* Alba House. New York. 1993.

Collectanea S. Congregationis de Propaganda Fidei seu Decreta Instructiones Rescripta pro Apostolicis Missionibus. Ex Typographia Polyglotta. Roma. 1907.

Congregation for the Doctrine of the Faith, "Note on the expression 'Sister Churches'", 30 June 2000 (http://www.vatican.va/roman_curia/congregations/cfaith/documents/rc_con_cfaith_doc_2000

0630_chiese-sorelle_en.html).
Cunningham, Francis. *The Christian Life*. Priory Press. Dubuque, Iowa. 1959.
Davis, Henry. *Moral and Pastoral Theology*. Sheed & Ward. New York. 1943.
Deferrari, Roy, J., ed. *A Latin-English Dictionary of St. Thomas Aquinas*. St. Paul Editions. Boston. 1986.
Denzinger, Henricus and Adulfus Schönmetzer. *Enchiridion Symbolorum: Definitionum et Declarationum de Rebus Fidei et Morum*. Herder. Friburg. 1976.
Dieckmann, Hermannus, S.J. *Theologia Fundamentalis: De Ecclesia*. Tomus I. Herder and Co. Friburgi Brisgoviae. 1925.
Edwards, Paul, ed. *The Encyclopedia of Philosophy*. MacMillan Publishing Co., Inc., and The Free Press. New York. 1972.
Fahey, Michael, S.J. *Orthodox and Catholic Sister Churches: East Is West and West Is East*. Marquette University Press. 1996.
----------------------"Am I My Sister's Keeper?" in America, 28 October 2000 (http://americamagazine.org/issue/386/article/am-i-my-sisters-keeper).
Garrigou-Lagrange, Reginald. *The Three Stages of the Interior Life: Prelude of Eternal Life*. TAN Books and Publishers, Inc. Rockford, Illinois. 1989.
Gilbert, P. Iosephus de, S.I. *De Christi Ecclesia: Breve Schema in Auditorum Usum*. Ed. Altera. Apud Aedes Universitatis Gregorianae. Roma. 1928.
Holy Bible. Douay Rheims Version. TAN Books and Publishers, Inc. Rockford, Illinois. 1989.
John Paul II. *Acting Person, The*. Originally published under his original name Karol Wojtyla. Trans. by Andrzej Potocki. D. Reidel Pub. Co. Dordrecht, Boston. 1979.
--------------. *Veritatis Splendor*. Acta Apostolicae Sedis. Vol. 85 (1993).
Jones, E. Michael. *Dionysos Rising : the Birth of Cultural Revolution out of the Spirit of Music*. Ignatius Press. San Francisco. 1994.
---------------------. *Living Machines : Bauhaus Architecture as Sexual Ideology*. Ignatius Press. San Francisco. 1995.
Journet, Charles. *The Church of the Word Incarnat: an Essay in Speculative Theology. Vol. I: The Apostolic Hierarchy*. Sheed and Ward. London and New York. 1955.
Leo XIII. *Satis Cognitum*. 1896.
Lutz, Petro. *Tractatus de Ecclesia Christi*. Woodstock College. Woodstock,

MD. 1924.

McHugh, John and Charles Callan. *Moral Theology; a Complete Course Based on St. Thomas Aquinas and the Best Modern Authorities.* J. F. Wagner, Inc. New York. 1929.

Noldin, H., S.J., *Summa Theologiae Moralis: De Principiis.* Vol. 1. Oeniponte, Innsbruck. 1956.

O'Donnell, Thomas. *Medicine and Christian Morality.* Alba House. Staten Island, New York. 1991.

Owen, Hugh. "The Traditional Catholic Doctrine of Creation." As found at http://kolbecenter.org/the-traditional-catholic-doctrine-of-creation/. December, 2017.

Ott, Ludwig. *Fundamentals of Catholic Dogma.* TAN Books and Publishers, Inc. Rockford, Illinois. 1974.

The Oxford Dictionary of the Christian Church. Oxford University Press. 2005.

Parente, Pietro. *Dictionary of Dogmatic Theology.* Bruce Publishing Company. Milwaukee, 1951.

Pesch, Christianus, S.J. *Institutiones Propaedeuticae ad Sacram Theologiam.* Ed. sexta et septima. Herder and Co. Friburgus. 1924.

Pius IX, *Tuas Libenter.* 1863.

Prummer, Dominicus, O.P. *Manuale Theologiae Moralis Secundum Principia S. Thomae Aquinatis.* Herder and Co. Friburgi. 1931.

Ramires, Jacobus, O.P. *De Actibus Humanis: in I-II Summae Theologiae Divi Thomae Expositio.* Instituto de Filosofia "Luis Vives." Madrid. 1972.

Revol, Fabian. *Le Temps de la Création.* Les Éditions du Cerf. Paris. 2015.

Ripperger, Chad. *Introduction to the Science of Mental Health.* Sensus Traditionis Press. 2013

--------------------. *Metaphysics of Evolution.* Books on Demand GmbH. 2012.

--------------------. "The Morality of the Exterior Act" as found in *Angelicum.* LXXVI (1999).

--------------------. *The Morality of the Exterior Act in the Writings of Saint Thomas Aquinas: Thesis ad Doctoratum in Philosophia totaliter edita.* Romae. 1996.

--------------------. "The Species and Unity of the Moral Act" as found in *The Thomist.* 59, 1, January, 1995.

Rituale Romanum. Benzinger Brothers. Chicago. 1947.

Robert F. Taft. "Perceptions and Realities in Orthodox–Catholic Relations Today". As found at http://fordham.universitypress scholarship.com/view/10.5422/fordham/9780823251926.001.

0001/upso-9780823251926-chapter-2 on 5/1/2018.
Thomas Aquinas. *Thomae Aquinatis Opera Omnia*. Iussu Impensaque Leonis XIII, edita. Roma: ex Typographia Polyglotta et al. 1882.
----------------------. *Summa Contra Gentiles*. trans. Anton Pegis. University of Notre Dame Press. 1975.
Vatican Council II: The Conciliarand Post Conciliar Documents. Austin Flannery, ed. Liturgical Press. Collegeville, Minnesota.1975.
Wuellner, Bernard J. *A Dictionary of Scholastic Philosophy*. Bruce Publishing Co. Milwaukee. 1966.
------------------------. *Summary of Scholastic Principles*. Loyola University Press. Chicago. 1956.

Printed in Great Britain
by Amazon